HAUNTED
MINING TOWNS
OF
ARIZONA

HAUNTED
MINING TOWNS
OF
ARIZONA

DARLENE WILSON AND PARKER ANDERSON

HAUNTED
America

Published by Haunted America
A Division of The History Press
Charleston, SC
www.historypress.com

This building was constructed by the Arizona Copper Company in the early 1900s, and then other companies occupied the building, including the Elks Lodge. It is now owned by the Town of Clifton. *Darlene Wilson.*
Castle Dome City, a ghost town and museum. The bells of this old historical church ring out to call people to church services. *Darlene Wilson.*

First published 2023

Manufactured in the United States

ISBN 9781467151887

Library of Congress Control Number: 2023937160

CONTENTS

ACKNOWLEDGEMENTS

W e want to thank the Sharlot Hall Museum Library and Archives for the information and pictures used in this book.
We'd also like to thank the Arizona State Library and Archives of Phoenix, Arizona

Thank you to the Arizona State Library and Archives for material on the United Verde Miners Hospital.

Thank you to Darlene's friends and investigating colleagues: Sandy Munz, Lisa Stephenson, Tom and Melissa Leeper, Maureen Riley, Linda Dershem and Dee Calhoon.

Thanks to Pamela Harrington and Erin Spears for sharing your stories and helping with the research on Clifton, Arizona.

Thanks to Karen and Matt Fry, the owners of the Clifton Hotel in Clifton, Arizona, for sharing your stories and photographs for this book; for preserving part of the history of your town; and for your constant generosity and friendship.

Thanks to Rita Olsen, the founder/owner of AZ Ghost Adventures, for sharing your stories on Miami and Globe, Arizona, and supporting local communities and their histories.

Thanks to Ken Mikell of the Harpy Trails for sharing your story of Jerome and the buildings sliding in 1936.

Thanks to Vincent Amico, the founder of the AZ Paranormal Investigation and Research Society, for sharing your stories, investigating with us and preserving Arizona's historic places.

Thanks to Molly Cornwell for sharing information on Globe, Arizona; assisting in our investigations at the Globe Train Station; and preserving the history and buildings of Globe.

Thanks to Tony Rathman, the founder and lead investigator of Entity Voices, for sharing your stories and photographs of the Phelps Dodge Hospital in Ajo.

A special thank-you to the owners and staff at the historical Palace Saloon and Restaurant for sharing your stories and photographs and allowing coauthor Darlene Wilson to bring groups of people into the saloon on her haunted tours. You always make us feel so welcome.

Thanks to historian, author and photographer Nancy Burgess for sharing your historical photographs and information for this book.

Thank you to all the wonderful people we met on our journey with this book. Everyone was so happy to share the history of their section of Arizona. What a wonderful experience it was meeting every one of you. You are in this book because you want the readers to know what was and is Arizona.

INTRODUCTION

President Abraham Lincoln signed the Organic Act on February 20, 1863, creating the Arizona Territory out of a portion of land that had been ceded by Mexico to the United States by force at the end of the Mexican-American War (1846–1848). More land was acquired through the Gadsden Purchase of 1853.

It took quite a few years for the United States to do much of anything with the land that would become Arizona. Some white men began trickling into the area, including an expedition through the Gadsden Purchase by Charles Debrille Poston and Herman Ehrenburg in late 1853. In 1856, Poston and Major Samuel Heintzelman set up the Sonora Exploring and Mining Company at the old Presidio of Tubac, which was likely Arizona's first mining operation. They were forced to flee when American troops were withdrawn to fight in the Civil War, and Apache attacks on them became common.

In the early 1860s, stray wildcat miners began staking small claims in the territory, but this changed after the Organic Act. Heavy mining started in earnest with the discovery of the richest gold strike in Arizona history by Henry Wickenburg, who named his mine the Vulture. Other rich strikes in those old days included those at Rich Hill in southern Yavapai County and Ed Schieffelin's strike at Tombstone. It was only a short time before mining became the Arizona Territory's primary source of income—from small mines to large operations from border to border. Strikes of gold, copper and silver were mined for many years.

Where mining hubs existed, towns grew up nearby to accommodate the needs of the miners. Businesses with food, liquor and other supplies were opened. Some of these mining towns had red-light districts, but contrary to popular belief, not all had ladies of the evening. In fact, in many mining towns, women were scarce, as many mining men had left their families elsewhere while they went off to seek their fortunes.

But by the 1930s, many decades after the first strikes, mining was starting to dry up in many areas of Arizona, with lode veins being tapped out and no new ones being discovered. So, the miners and mining operations left those areas, leaving entire towns abandoned permanently. Some mining towns survived the end of mining (though they shrank in size), but many more did not. Arizona has many ghost towns, most of which were once bustling with business and mining activity. Today, mining continues in parts of Arizona but is less widespread than it was in the late nineteenth and early twentieth centuries.

For those who believe in ghosts, is it not reasonable to think that many of the working miners of old may have stuck around after their deaths, their spirits frequenting the areas that were so important to them in life? Arizona's mining towns, both those that have survived and those that have not, have long had reports of paranormal activity. In this book, Darlene Wilson and Parker Anderson explore some of these towns, their histories and their haunted activities.

WHAT HAPPENS TO US after we die? This is a question mankind has been asking since the beginning of time, and there has never been a consensus. The belief in what occurs following death differs from culture to culture and from era to era, with the only consistency being that we have a soul that goes *somewhere* after our inevitable demise.

So, what about ghosts or spirits? These terms are often used interchangeably, but they do have distinct meanings.

A ghost is typically considered to be the spirit of a deceased person that has not yet moved on to the afterlife. They can appear in the form of an apparition, an orb or an entirely transparent person. What remains here when someone dies? Their essence or higher self?

Spirit is a broader term that can refer to any nonphysical entity or essence. This can include deceased humans' spirits and other entities such as angels, demons or spirit guides.

Orbs are the most controversial objects you can capture in photographs. They can be spirit beings or dust particles flying around. You have to be aware of your surroundings to decide whether it is a ghost or dust. An orb is one way a ghost/spirit can show itself. It takes less energy to show up as an orb. That's why you might see more orbs than apparitions.

Many believe that ghosts are the spirits of the dead, remaining behind in places they love. Others believe these spirits are trapped in some vortex because they died horrible deaths on a particular property. Still others think the ghosts are not related to the property but have settled there because they like the area. All of this could be true. It is unlikely that one explanation covers every lingering spirit. These reasons could be as varied as the spirits themselves.

Ghost sightings and haunted places are so widespread that virtually every sizable town and city in the world, whether abandoned or active, has them. What is responsible for these phenomena is a matter of debate. There are many differing opinions about the meaning of ghosts and spirits and what happens to us after we die. Our advice is to read everything you can about any paranormal subject you are interested in and then form your own opinion. Don't believe everything you read and hear—only what feels right to you.

Northwest Arizona

Cerbat

Cerbat was a mining town located in the Cerbat Mountains. Today, it is a complete ghost town, though at one time, it was prosperous enough that it was the third county seat of Mohave County.

Mining began here shortly after Arizona first achieved territorial status in 1864. Cerbat was soon home to enough individual miners and their families

The mining town of Cerbat at its peak in the 1880s. Today, only a few abandoned buildings remain. *Sharlot Hall Museum.*

that a post office was opened in 1872. The town had all the amenities of its day, including merchants, a school, a doctor's office and saloons.

But success is fleeting, and by the start of the twentieth century, Cerbat was already beginning to die out. The post office was officially closed in 1912.

Today, there are some old buildings still standing in a derelict condition that are very interesting to visit, though the road to the ghost town is rough. No one lives here anymore. The town cemetery is reportedly still accessible, although during a visit in 2013, Parker Anderson and some friends were unable to locate it, despite having directions on how to reach it.

The Cerbat ruins have generally not been targets of paranormal investigators, although visitors have reported experiencing eerie sensations in the old buildings.

CLARKDALE

Clarkdale was founded as a company town in 1912 by mining magnate William A. Clark to house the miners working in his United Verde operation up in Jerome. Clark made sure his town had all the new modern amenities, such as electricity and running water.

As the mine employed a lot of Mexican labor, Clarkdale was originally a segregated town, with its Latino residents restricted to certain areas. But when the United Verde Mine permanently closed in 1953, Clarkdale fell on very hard times, as did Jerome. It survived largely due to the few residents who remained and succeeded in incorporating the town in 1957, and in 1959, the Phoenix Cement Company opened a plant a few miles from town, which helped partially revitalize Clarkdale's economy. The plant still operates.

Today, Clarkdale is largely a retirement community, and like Jerome, it has seen a good bit of growth in recent years. Its economy is helped by the Verde Canyon Railroad, which offers train rides to tourists, as well as the Tuzigoot National Monument, an old Sinagua ruin that was donated to the National Park Service by Phelps Dodge in 1938. The Verde River is a popular kayaking and fishing destination and a great spot for wildlife viewing. The town is also home to a variety of wildlife, including coyotes, deer, javelinas and wild turkeys. The area is also popular for camping, hiking and off-roading.

Clarkdale's two surviving school buildings are said to be haunted. Both schools are long closed, and the grade school building is not in use and largely boarded up. Those who have been inside the grade school have reported hearing strange sounds and seeing shadows out of the corners of their eyes. The old high school building is now the Copper Art Museum, which displays various pieces of artwork and sculptures crafted out of copper.

The old Clark mansion, built by William Clark III (the grandson of William Andrews Clark), was long a landmark in town and had a similarly eerie reputation until it was destroyed by fire in 2010. The fire was listed by authorities as "suspicious."

Clarkdale, Arizona, is said to be home to a few hauntings. One of the most popular ghostly tales is that of the ghostly woman who haunts the abandoned Clarkdale Jail. Witnesses have reported seeing an apparition of a woman in a long dress hovering around the jail between midnight and dawn.

The town infirmary and jail is now home to the Clarkdale Historical Society and Museum. One has to wonder what they have experienced.

The Ghost Bell Lady of Clarkdale, Arizona, is a local legend that can be traced back to the early 1900s. The Ghost Bell Lady is a popular figure in Clarkdale and has been the subject of many stories and urban legends.

Clarkdale Smelter. *Nancy Burgess.*

Decoration Day in Clarkdale in 1917. *Nancy Burgess.*

Some believe that she is the spirit of a woman who worked as a nurse in the nearby copper smelter, while others believe that she was a railroad worker who was killed while trying to cross the tracks. Still others believe that the Ghost Bell Lady is the spirit of a miner who was killed in a cave-in in the nearby mines.

Whatever the true story behind the Ghost Bell Lady may be, it is clear that she has become an important part of the folklore of Clarkdale. People often report hearing her ringing her bell late at night, usually near the train tracks. Some people have even reported seeing her ghostly figure walking along the tracks. It is a reminder of the people who lived, worked and died in the area—and of the stories that have been passed down through the generations.

The haunted bridge near Clarkdale, Arizona, has been a local legend for many years. The bridge is located on Old Jerome Highway and is said to be the site of several strange occurrences. Witnesses have reported seeing the ghost of a girl standing on the bridge in the middle of the night and have heard her voice calling for help.

Other stories about the bridge include reports of mysterious lights and noises coming from the area, as well as eerie feelings experienced by those who have ventured near it.

Congress

In Southern Yavapai County, not far from the Maricopa County line, is the town of Congress. And close by are the ghost towns of Stanton, Octave and Weaver. This entire section of Arizona came to be inhabited due to gold mining. The bonanza gold strike on Rich Hill started it all in the 1860s, and soon, other miners staked their claims in the surrounding area.

The claim that would later become the Congress Mine was staked circa 1883 by Dennis May, who had a number of other less successful claims in the area. This claim, however, was producing enough gold that May had to fend off bids to buy him out. One popular area legend contends that he bravely declined an offer to sell the claim to the villainous Charles P. Stanton (see later section). This story has no documentation.

In 1889, however, Dennis May sold his mine to James Reynolds, nicknamed "Diamond Jim," an East Coast businessman who had the money and resources to increase development at the mine. It was he who named it the Congress Mine—for reasons that are not entirely clear. Soon, the Congress Mine became one of the busiest gold mines in the Arizona Territory, churning out millions of dollars in gold and employing over four hundred men.

The miners working the Congress needed a place to live, so houses and stores started appearing at the mine site. Prior to Diamond Jim Reynolds acquiring everything, the small town was reportedly named Martinez. A post office was added, and with this, the town was officially named Congress.

The Congress Gold Mine Company changed hands after the sudden death of Diamond Jim Reynolds, and it was purchased by a group of

Congress Mine in the early twentieth century. Its riches were once so famous that President William McKinley visited the site. *Nancy Burgess.*

investors, including Frank Murphy, an associate of Diamond Jim who had been fighting hard to get the railroad to come through or near Congress. This dream was realized in the 1890s, when Congress became a major stop on the rail line between Prescott and Phoenix.

During this time, new homes and businesses were being built a few miles south of Congress, and this development was named Congress Junction. Today, however, it is this area that is named Congress.

The Congress Mine was important enough in the Arizona Territory that in 1901, William McKinley, the president of the United States, paid a visit. Photographs of his tour of the mine still survive.

But like most profitable mines of the era, the Congress Mine eventually played itself out and closed in 1910. Most of the residents moved either far away or to neighboring Congress Junction. Arizona became a state on February 14, 1912.

The small burg of Congress Junction survived and was given a boost in the 1920s, when U.S. Highway 89 was routed through there, making the town a nice rest stop for travelers in the days before Interstate 17 bypassed it all (between Phoenix and Prescott) in the 1970s. The day came when "Junction" was dropped from the community's name, and what you drive through today is simply known as Congress.

Congress has experienced a new boom within the last twenty-five years or so. Mining has started again, at least on a smaller scale, at the old mine site, and the area's population is rapidly growing, even as you read this, along with that of much of Arizona.

Congress Pioneer Cemetery

Although Congress does not have a reputation for much paranormal activity, the town has two cemeteries near the old mine. The residential road leading out toward to the mine is appropriately named Ghost Town Road. The cemeteries are located on dirt roads that turn off Ghost Town Road. The oldest one, the Congress Pioneer Cemetery, has only a few marked graves and many unmarked ones, and it undoubtedly contains the graves of many of the men who worked the Congress Mine.

The old Congress Pioneer Cemetery contains the grave of Idaho miner Ben Caswell, who died in 1937. In the 1890s, Ben and his brothers Lew and Dan located the Thunder Mountain gold claim in Idaho, setting off a major gold rush there. Ben later moved to Congress, where he died, though it is a mystery why his body was not returned to his native Idaho for burial. An even bigger mystery was why he was buried in the Pioneer Cemetery (which had been closed to burials by then) instead of the newer Congress Cemetery (see the following section).

Due to the remoteness of its location, the Congress Pioneer Cemetery does seem to exude an eerie atmosphere and is sometimes visited by paranormal investigators' "cemetery crawls."

Congress Cemetery

The main Congress Cemetery is nearby, though not in view of the Pioneer Cemetery. It is very old as well; its oldest graves date to the early twentieth century. This cemetery is still in use today.

Among those buried here is Harry M. Anderson, who once served as mayor of Hillsboro, North Dakota (1937–41). In his retirement years, Anderson moved to Congress and started a new family. Interred next to him are the cremains of his wife, Darla, and son Pembrook.

Martinez Cemetery

There is some evidence there was another cemetery in the area, the Martinez Cemetery, in the days before everything in the area was renamed Congress. Some people believe this is the same burial ground known as the Congress Pioneer Cemetery today. In Parker Anderson's earlier book *Cemeteries of Yavapai County* (Charleston, SC: Arcadia Publishing, 2013), he said as much, but this may have been an error.

The one known photograph of Martinez Cemetery (reposited at Sharlot Hall Museum in Prescott) shows a burial ground that strongly resembles the Pioneer Cemetery, except for a dry riverbed beside it. The Pioneer Cemetery is not located by a river. Old handwriting on the back of the photograph states that the Martinez Cemetery was washed away in a flood at some point.

If there was indeed a separate Martinez Cemetery that is no longer extant, its location is unknown today.

Mysterious Tunnels?

On July 15, 1951, an unusual article appeared in the *Arizona Republic* newspaper contending that a series of underground tunnels had been discovered underneath the ruins of the now-abandoned town of Congress near the mine. The article was written by Roscoe G. Willson, a sage who penned a folksy history column in the *Arizona Republic* from the 1940s to the 1960s.

In this column, Willson claimed to have interviewed a man named Larry J. Kerwin, who had recently purchased the ruins of old Congress. Many of the town's old buildings were still there, boarded up and left largely undisturbed since the mine had closed. He admitted to discarding a lot of old mining ledgers, lanterns, old books, et cetera, items that would be considered valuable today, but historic preservation was not an issue in 1951.

Kerwin told Willson that while cleaning out the old Martinez Mercantile building, he discovered the entrances to two underground tunnels in the basement. While exploring them, he found turns to numerous other tunnels and speculated they ran under the entire ghost town. He further stated that he found artifacts in the tunnels, including Chinese clothing, Yaqui arrows and three vials of coarse gold.

In a commentary that probably would not sit well with today's social values, Willson speculated that the tunnels were used to smuggle Chinese men from Mexico in the late nineteenth and early twentieth centuries and as an escape route in case things got too hot for them in town (never mind that Congress is far away from the Mexican border).

Roscoe Willson's article seems to be the only source for the idea that there were tunnels under the original Congress town site. All the old buildings have since been bulldozed. With nothing more to go on, one may speculate that property owner Larry Kerwin was telling tall tales to get attention (Willson's column closes with the notation that Kerwin was trying to resell the property).

A number of Arizona towns have legends of "Chinese tunnels" underneath them, most notably Prescott, Williams and Winslow. None of these legends have been verified, and they never explain how the itinerant Chinese immigrants of the day could have excavated lengthy, structurally sound tunnels without attracting considerable attention. Yet these stories have their supporters, so they live on.

CROWN KING

The former gold mining town of Crown King is another town that defied the odds after the mining ended, and it still exists with a very small but active population. Located deep in the Southern Bradshaw Mountains, Crown King today is accessible by difficult gravel roads.

Reportedly, the first individual gold mining claim filed here was called the Buckeye Mine, and it was filed by one Rod McKinnon in 1875. More followed, and soon, as usual, a town sprang up around the mining activity. The town was originally called Crowned King, named after one of the mines that bore the same name, but the name was later shortened to Crown King. At one time, the town had stores, restaurants and, despite the remoteness of its location, electricity in those early days.

Beginning in 1904, Crown King was serviced by the Bradshaw Mountain Railroad, a train line from Mayer that wound up the rocky terrain to the town. This railroad was financed by Frank M. Murphy, an Arizona businessman who had investments in a widely diverse array of projects in his lifetime. As the mining started to peter out, this rail line was abandoned in 1926. Today, the main road to Crown King from Interstate-17 utilizes part of the old railroad bed.

Today, Crown King survives, its economy based mostly on tourism, which it gets despite its remoteness and how difficult it is to reach it. Its current population is around 177, but it still holds a small general store for residents (which contains the post office), two restaurants, a library and a school. Some years, the school has had fewer than five students, but it stays open because the remoteness of Crown King makes it impossible to bus the children to Mayer, the closest town with a school. Living in Crown King is not like living in any other small town—it is a way of life.

Crown King Quartz Mine. *Nancy Burgess.*

Countess Agnes Minotto

Agnes Sorma was a famed European stage actress in the mid-nineteenth and early twentieth centuries, appearing in a variety of sophisticated plays across the European continent. Some sources say she was the first actress to portray Nora in a production of Henrik Ibsen's *A Doll's House*, but this is unproven. She eventually married an Italian count, Demetrius Minotto, and became a countess. When her husband died in 1920, Countess Agnes Minotto moved to—of all places—Crown King, Arizona.

The Minottos' son, James, led a colorful life as a banker, an international diplomat for the U.S. government and a rancher in Yavapai County. He also participated in the annual July Fourth rodeo in Prescott. He inherited the title of count from his father but never used it.

When Countess Agnes Minotto died in 1926, she was initially buried in Crown King, but later, James had her remains disinterred and reburied next to those of his father in Germany. James was also one of the original founders of the Prescott Area Arts and Humanities Council (PAAHC). He died in 1980 and was buried in Skull Valley, Arizona, alongside the graves of other family members.

One evening, during one of Darlene Wilson's Haunted Prescott Tours, Wilson had a couple on the tour who lived in the mountains in Prescott. She did not know precisely where they lived, but she knew they had no internet or cable service there. The man told Wilson that when he was very young, he, his parents and his grandparents lived in Crown King in what was once the barn just down the hill from the main house. One day, his grandmother went out to tend to the animals, and when she opened the front door, she found a very tall man standing there. He was in buckskins from head to foot and was holding a long rifle. She screamed, and he disappeared. Ten years later, his mother went out to feed the chickens, and when she opened the door, she saw a tall man wearing buckskin from head to toe standing there and holding a long rifle. She screamed, and he disappeared. Who was this man who showed up at their door? They believe it was the original owner of the main house.

Another story that is shared today is about one of the mines in the area. According to local lore, the mine is haunted by the spirit of a miner who was killed by a cave-in. People who venture near the mine report hearing the miner moaning in pain and feeling a cold chill in the air.

Like many stories about these mining towns, this story has been passed down through many generations, and regardless of whether they are true, they are interesting. Just knowing how difficult mining was in those days, you know there are ghosts that still linger in these places. Strange and unexplained things do happen.

JEROME

High on Cleopatra Hill above the Verde Valley in Central Yavapai County is the town of Jerome. It is a striking town to see, with homes, businesses and streets clinging precariously to the steep side of the mountain. Yet the town has been there since 1876 with no major incidents of buildings sliding down, though the town burned and was rebuilt several times in the late nineteenth century. Jerome was once home to two of the richest copper claims in Arizona history.

The first mining claims in the area were filed by prospectors Marion A. Ruffner and Angus McKinnon in 1876, although four years later, they were bought out by future Arizona territorial governor Frederick Tritle and his business partners. (Tritle was the first governor with his business interests to have ties to Arizona before assuming office.)

Tritle and his partners, with financing from wealthy New York City businessmen James MacDonald and Eugene Jerome, formed the United Verde Copper Company. As with all active mining operations at the time, a

Jerome Main Street in the 1920s. *Nancy Burgess.*

An interior photograph of the smelter in Jerome, where they would pour copper. *Nancy Burgess.*

small town grew up nearby, this one on the side of the mountain next to the United Verde. It was named for Eugene Jerome.

But copper prices fell around 1884, and the United Verde closed its operations. In stepped controversial Montana businessman and politician William Andrews Clark, who had made his vast fortune mining in his home state and was one of the richest men in the world. He purchased the United Verde, reopened it, enlarged its smelter and constructed a railroad to go west of Jerome for easy transfer of ore that was being shipped out. During its existence, the United Verde Copper Company was said to have extracted over thirty-three million tons of ore.

The increased activity at the United Verde Mine caused the town of Jerome to grow considerably, and incredible as it seems today, at its peak, it housed nearly twenty thousand people. Jerome had businesses, churches and fraternal organizations, but as was the case with so many mining towns, vice conditions existed, as the mining men, after long days and weeks of work, sought out gambling, prostitutes and liquor. The town developed a high crime rate, and Yavapai County authorities had their hands full much of the time with the town of Jerome.

By 1914, miner and businessman James S. "Rawhide Jimmy" Douglas located a second large ore body of copper near Jerome and created the UVX (short for United Verde Extension) Mining Company. Douglas had mining interests around Arizona, and the mining town of Douglas, by the Mexican border, was named for him. He was also the father of future U.S. ambassador to Britain Lewis Douglas, and the Douglas mansion in Jerome is now a State Historic Site.

World War I caused a nationwide demand for copper, and the two rival mining companies increased production dramatically. The United

Verde eventually stopped smelting and began open pit operations at its site while simultaneously building its own company town, Clarkdale (named for William Andrews Clark), below the mountains. Meanwhile, the UVX formed its own company town, Clemenceau, named in honor of the French premier Georges Clemenceau, continuing an unofficial pattern in Yavapai County of naming towns after men who had nothing to do with the area (including Prescott, Humboldt and Dewey). Later on, Clememceau was absorbed by neighboring Cottonwood, so it no longer exists as a town.

With the increasing influence of labor unions in America, many of the men working in the Jerome mines became unionized, and during the 1910s, there were a number of violent strikes. But prosperous times returned in the 1920s, and Jerome continued to grow. William A. Clark died in 1925, but his family continued to operate the United Verde.

The Great Depression hit hard in the 1930s, and mining was greatly reduced or ended completely throughout the state of Arizona. The price of copper plummeted dramatically, and the United Verde significantly reduced its workforce and output, and the Clark family finally sold the mine to Phelps Dodge in 1935 (although mining is no longer carried out in Jerome, Phelps Dodge still owns most of the land). Meanwhile, Rawhide Jimmy Douglas's UVX Mining Company ceased operations in 1938 and closed down permanently.

In 1936, the T.F. Miller building was the company store, and at some point, it became one of Jerome's largest stores. Today, it is Spook Hall and the community center for Jerome. In 1936, about 1.8 to 2.4 tons of dynamite accidentally exploded, and a massive shockwave hit the town. The three blocks between the Bartlet Hotel and the Bordello Restaurant began to shift and slide down the mountain at the rate of about four inches a day. The buildings began to break up, which began the sliding jail's two-hundred-foot journey down the hill. The photograph on the following page was taken about halfway through the slide, when the buildings began breaking up.

Phelps Dodge continued minimal mining operations in the United Verde until 1953, when they closed the mine. As with most mining towns, in Jerome, when the mining ended, the population evaporated. Once home to twenty thousand people, Jerome became a ruin of old, decrepit, boarded-up buildings with a population of fewer than one hundred.

The end of mining in many parts of Arizona completely wiped out scores of small towns, many of which have nothing left and are complete ghost towns. The few residents left in Jerome were determined to not let that happen

Top: Jerome's Main Street in 1936. You can see a collapsed building from an accidental dynamite explosion. *Nancy Burgess.*

Bottom: Jerome's famous sign depicting its rapidly decreasing population after the mines closed. *Nancy Burgess.*

to their home. They began marketing the town to tourists, promoting it as a "lively" ghost town. This campaign had modest success, as tourists came to check the town out. This kept Jerome from dying out completely, and the campaign of "Arizona's Liveliest Ghost Town" kept going through the 1970s. The town's residents succeeded in obtaining National Historic Landmark status for Jerome in 1967. By the 1980s, Jerome had some modest growth again, but this was not due to mining. Today, the town has a population of about five hundred and has art galleries, wineries, restaurants and museums to attract visitors. It is a thriving little town once again on its own merits instead of the mining industry's.

In 2013, before same-sex marriage was legalized throughout America, Jerome was the third town in Arizona (after Tucson and Bisbee) to recognize same-sex "civil unions." Jerome was also, for many years, the home of legendary folk singer and environmental activist Katie Lee.

Jerome Grand Hotel

With its checkered and violent history, Jerome is bound to be haunted, and some have said it is perhaps the most haunted town in Arizona. Many buildings in the town have ghosts; they are mostly benign, but a few are reportedly hostile. One of the best-known haunted sites in town is the Jerome Grand Hotel. This luxurious and quaint hotel was once the United Verde Miners' Hospital. It is no wonder that it is haunted, with its history of mining-related accidents, disease and agonizing death.

The hotel is considered one of the paranormal hot spots in the much-haunted Jerome. Incidents of guests waking up to strange noises and lights being turned on and off are common. Jerome Grand Hotel has been profiled on a number of ghost hunter TV programs and podcasts. Some have felt the ghostly presences are sinister, owing to the large number of unnatural deaths that occurred due to mining accidents.

Locals believe that one of the primary ghosts that haunts the Jerome Grand Hotel is that of Claude Harvey, who local legend says died mysteriously in the United Verde Hospital after being crushed in the basement by the service elevator. Unlike many hotel hauntings in America, where there is no documentation for some of the ghostly backstories, this one happens to be mostly true.

Claude McLeod Harvey was a Scottish immigrant who worked as a boilermaker in the United Verde Mining Hospital starting in 1914. In

UNITED VERDE HOSPITAL. JEROME. ARIZONA

Jerome United Verde Hospital in the early twentieth century. It is now the renovated Grand Hotel and is regarded as one of the most haunted sites in Jerome. *Nancy Burgess.*

the very early morning of April 3, 1935, he was found crushed to death under the hospital's service elevator. His death was viewed as very odd, with unanswered questions about why Harvey was in the elevator shaft to begin with and why he did not notice the elevator coming down the shaft above him. Some wondered—and still wonder today—if he was murdered and his body placed in the shaft to destroy evidence of foul play.

Upon the discovery of his body, only minutes after the purported accident occurred, a coroner's inquest jury was called to determine his cause of death (a practice rarely used any more). Jerome's justice of the peace Frank E. Smith presided over the proceedings. The Jerome citizens called to serve on the coroner's jury were identified as J.G. Crowley, J.P. Connolly, H.W. Eldridge, E.E. McFarland, J.S. Prosser and Henry Weigand. Judge Smith questioned all the witnesses.

The transcript of the coroner's inquest on the death of Claude Harvey has survived, but despite modern-day interest in his tragic death, it seems to never have been published before.

The first witness to testify was hospital employee John Zivkovich, who found Harvey's body.

> *Q. What is your name, occupation and residence?*
> *A. John Zivkovich, working at the hospital and living in Jerome.*
> *Q. You were present there this morning, and at what time did the accident occur?*
> *A. Could not swear to the exact time. Think about twenty minutes to seven the last time I saw him. It was before seven.*
> *Q. Were you there all night?*

A. Yes.

Q. When were you first aware there was something wrong with the elevator?

A. Miss Morton came down and said the elevator was making a noise and seemed to be out of order, and would I see Mr. Harvey about fixing it. I thought he was in the kitchen, but he was not there, and I looked for him. I saw a light over by the elevator, so I stepped over there and saw him laying under the elevator as you gentlemen saw him.

Q. You have taken his place?

A. I am now.

Q. Will it be part of your duty to take care of the elevator?

A. Not exactly. If something goes wrong, I can call someone to do it.

Q. Was it part of his duty to take care of the elevator?

A. We should take care of the oiling of the elevator.

Q. You did not know he was there?

A. No.

Q. When did you last see him alive?

A. About twenty minutes of seven was the last time I saw him alive.

Q. When you found him, as you say, what time was that?

A. Could not say exactly—possibly three minutes later.

Q. Three minutes after you first saw him until you found him dead? I thought you went upstairs after you last saw him alive.

Q. Where were you when you last saw him alive?

A. In his room. I talked to him, and we just had time to get our breakfast. I went to get my overalls, and just then, the girl came.

Q. That was about twenty minutes to seven?

A. Yes.

Q. And it was only about three minutes after that?

A. Yes, about three minutes from the time I left his room until he must have died, I just went for my overalls.

Q. Have you any opinion as to the cause of the accident?

A. I have no opinion. [I] could not say what was the cause.

Q. What was the position of the body?

A. His head was under the elevator with his shoulders sticking out. His body was hunched up, and he was laying on his face, and the elevator was on his neck. When I saw that, I went and told the girl, and she went and called Mr. Henson, and he was laying in the same position when he saw him.

Q. Did you and Mr. Henson move the body?

A. No, we were waiting for the doctor.

Q. From what you say of the position of the body, did you think the cage came down on him?

A. I don't see how.

Q. What did you think?

A. I only thought the cage came down while he was looking at something, then accidentally struck him.

Q. Then you think it struck him?

A. Don't see how else.

Q. You think it was an accident?

A. It must have been an accident, or he could see it.

Judge Smith. Has the jury any questions?

Mr. Connolly. Would it be possible, if he were standing on his feet, for it to hit him on the head?

Judge Smith. That will be for the jury to decide.

Mr. Eldredge. How did the cage happen to come down?

A. I don't know how if somebody called it or not. I did not see anybody around the elevator, and it was making a funny noise.

Mr. Connolly. Will it travel with the door open?

A. No.

Mr. Connolly. Has anybody tampered with the door?

A. I don't know.

Mr. Crowley. Does the elevator move very slowly?

A. Yes, very slow.

Mr. McFarland. Could the elevator have been started from the level he was on?

A. No.

Mr. Riordan. Mr. Henson can answer such questions when he is on the stand.

Zivkovich was excused, and T.C. Henson was sworn in.

Q. State your name, residence and occupation.

A. T.C. Henson, 31 Magnolia Avenue, Jerome, Arizona. Electrician foreman for Upper Verde Public Utilities.

Q. I am not going to question you much. Think it would be better for you to go ahead and tell the jury in your own words all you know.

A. About 6:45, the phone rang, and I jumped out of bed to answer it. I glanced at the clock, as I thought I might have overslept and someone was calling to find out if I was coming to work. Miss Morton was on the phone and said that something was wrong with the elevator and that she thought someone was fastened under it, so I dressed as quickly as possible and ran to the hospital. Mr. Zivkovich was there. He took me right in, and I saw Mr. Harvey there, and the motor was still running, so I ran to cut the current and threw the switch to try and get him out as quickly as possible. Dr. Gaede came right in to examine for life, which he did very quickly. Then I was over my fright and began to work the controls to raise the elevator off Mr. Harvey, so I raised it, pressing the button. Then I was afraid it might set the cage lower and do more damage. By using both hands, [I] managed the controls and raised it a little, and Dr. Gaede and I dragged him out and left him as the jury found him. Then I locked the switch open and left.

Q. *What position was he in when you saw him first?*

A. *His body was on the stomach with head out of sight, as if he might have been looking down the sump, was my first opinion.*

Q. *You could not see his head?*

A. *Could not see his head for the reason the cage was resting on it.*

Q. *How had [the] cage struck in your opinion?*

A. *I have said that it was possible that he was looking down into the sump.*

Q. *How far below is the sump?*

A. *The sump is about three and a half to four feet below.*

Q. *When you first saw the body, the cage was resting on the head of the deceased?*

A. *It was.*

Q. *Have you any theory of your own as to how it was brought about?*

A. *I couldn't say, but my first impression was that it was possible that I might have been looking down the shaft to find the trouble. Later on, it was apparent that there was a cut on top of the head, and I thought he might have been standing up listening, as I have done myself. When Dr. Carlson washed off the blood, there was only a small wound just behind the right ear a little to the center.*

Q. *What rested on the back of the neck?*

A. *The elevator cage.*

Q. *You had no suspicion of foul play?*

A. *No.*

Q. *Did you conclude from appearances that it was an accident?*

A. *I did.*

Judge Smith (to jury). Any questions?

Mr. Crowley. Would he have had any work in and around there?

A. *Yes, in general line of duty, there were some places to grease and to look after it generally, and if he thought it needed anything special, he was to call a mechanic, but I think it was the engineer's duty to look after it all the time.*

Q. Then you think the unfortunate man had a right to be there?

A. Yes.

Judge Smith (to jury). Have you any further questions?

Mr. Riordan. Was anyone on the elevator when you got there?

A. No.

Q. How did the elevator get there in your opinion?

A. Apparently, someone pushed the button and called it to the basement.

Mr. Eldridge. Could the elevator have been worked from where the deceased was found?

A. I could work it from down there, but none of the men up there know how. It is a case of knowing how to move it in an emergency. I use two sticks to manipulate the switch.

Q. Are you positive he did not know how to start it?

A. Yes, I am positive.

Q. And equally positive someone from above started it?

A. No, I am not positive of that.

Dr. Carlson. Is it not absolutely positive that it had to be started from that floor?

A. Yes, unless something was wrong with the elevator.

Dr. Carlson. Nothing more—just that question.

Mr. Riordan. Could Mr. Harvey have called the elevator to the basement and have walked down there by the time the elevator got there?

A. Yes, there would have been lots of time, if on an upper floor, to be there before it got there.

Henson was then excused, and Gladys Morton, the nurse, was called to the stand.

Q. Please give your name, residence and occupation.

A. Gladys Morton, nurse at the hospital, live at the hospital.

Q. I am told you originally discovered something wrong with the elevator and went to give the information.

A. I did.

Q. Please tell the jury in your own way what happened.

A. I discovered something wrong with the elevator at twenty minutes of seven when I went to tell them to turn on the steam, as we were going to operate this morning. The elevator was making a noise, so I told John to find Mr. Harvey. He started to find Mr. Harvey and found him there.

Q. Were you the one who originally found him?

A. *I think I was the second. John was first.*

Q. *When you saw him, what position was he in, with relation to face or back?*

A. *On his face with his head under the cage.*

Q. *You could not see his head?*

A. *No I could not.*

Q. *You think it is possible the cage came down and caught him?*

A. *Yes.*

Dr. Carlson. *Where was the cage the last time you knew of its location?*

A. *At five after six, the cage was on the fourth floor, but I heard the cage going up or down after that while I was at my desk. I did not pay any attention to where it might be going. When I went to call it, I noticed it was humming.*

Q. *Then you went down at that time to see what was wrong?*

A. *Yes.*

Dr. Carlson. *Did you hear Mr. Harvey moan?*

A. *No, not moan.*

Mr. Crowley. *Does the cage run very slowly?*

A. *Yes.*

Mr. Connolly. *To your knowledge, would it have been possible for anyone to have moved it?*

A. *Yes, from any floor, by pressing the button, it is possible to go to any floor called with the door closed.*

Q. *Did you assist in moving the body?*

A. *No I did not. Mattie came a little later. Perhaps it was her.*

At that point, Dr. Menno S. Gaede, who first examined the body, was sworn in.

Q. *What is your name, occupation and residence?*

A. *Dr. Menno S. Gaede. Physician, house 35, Company Hill, Jerome.*

Q. *Please tell the jurors, Doctor, all you know about this death that occurred.*

A. *I was called by phone by Mrs. Lyle at ten minutes to seven and got there five minutes later, so Mrs. Lyle told me, and was immediately taken back into the engine room, where Mr. Harvey was found, head pinned under the elevator, prone position, legs extended, left arm under chest, right hand close to face. He did not show any signs of life. I removed the left arm to get [the] stethoscope close to heart, found no heart beats and no breath sounds in lungs. After I had examined Mr. Harvey, the cage was moved, and I pulled Mr. Harvey back about eighteen inches to further examine him, grabbing his belt with my right hand; under the head, I put my left hand. [I] found a streak of blood in the middle of the forehead from [a] scratch. There was a cut [on the] back of the right ear, blood coming from [the] nose and [it] had also run into [his] mouth. The right hand was also paler in color than the left hand, apparently due to pressure. That is about all I observed.*

Q. Other witnesses have previously testified the man was killed by having been struck by descending cage. Is this your belief?

A. Yes. Probably pressure on back of neck was immediate cause of death.

Q. Was [the] neck broken?

A. That cannot be determined without an X-ray. I did not move the neck in such manner as to determine that, as pressure over that area would cause almost immediate death.

Q. You believe that to have been the cause of death?

A. Yes.

Q. From your observations, other than medical examination, you believe from all appearances that death was accidental?

A. It appears to be an accident, although a very peculiar one.

Judge Smith. Dr. Carlson, have you any questions?

Dr. Carlson. One thing, I would like to explain the position of the hospital, and could I ask Mr. Zivkovich one question?

John Zivkovich was then recalled to the stand.

Dr. Carlson. Did you press the button to bring the cage down?

A. No.

Dr. A.C. Carlson, the company physician, was then called to give the official position of United Verde Copper Company.

Dr. Carlson. In this hospital, the elevator cannot be moved except to push a button to call it to a floor, unless the button is pushed by someone in the elevator, and it will then move with the door closed. We know there was nobody in the elevator, and when the door is opened, the motor stops. When Mr. Harvey was found, there was no one in the elevator, and the motor was going. There was no one on duty in the hospital besides Miss Morton and Mrs. Vivian Harrington, except the cook and dishwasher, who were busy with breakfast. The doctors and porters arrive later. It was too early for any schoolchild to have played a prank. Mr. Zivkovich says that he did not start the elevator, and if it is possible that anyone else did and found that an accident had occurred, [they would] would not go away. I believe that Mr. Harvey actually brought that elevator to that floor, regardless of how. For, as I say, there was no one there but Miss Morton, Mrs. Harrington and the cook and dishwasher.

Judge Smith. Are there any questions?

Mr. Crowley. In your opinion, would he have had time to press the button and walk around?

A. I believe so. Mr. Henson says he believes so if the elevator was on the third or fourth floor and you wanted to, as the movement is very slow up as well as down.

Q. If Mr. Harvey had started the elevator, could he have done so from the position in which he was found?

A. According to Mr. Henson, he could, but Mr. Harvey did not know how, and I have no knowledge of it. If John did not do it, there was no one else around, and Mr. Harvey must have moved the elevator.

T.C. Henson was recalled to clarify his earlier testimony.

Mr. Henson. Relative to moving the cage, Doctor, there are three sets of contacts you must hold, and a man must insulate himself. You see it is about this high [Mr. Henson illustrates], too high for Mr. Harvey to have operated it from where he was found. He would have had to operate it from this side and then move around. He would have had to move about six or eight feet. The switch board is about three feet wide, and he would have had to be on the extreme right-hand corner to reach the switch.

Q. Then it was possible for the deceased to start the elevator and get back into position?

A. Yes, it would be possible for anyone who knew how, but we have kept it secret, as it is very dangerous. Nobody has ever been shown.

Q. But he could have pushed the button on the outside and get around.

Mr. Riordan. Mr. Henson and Fred and I demonstrated that it could be done. There is plenty of time to push the button and get back to where he was found, especially if the elevator should be on the third or fourth floor. We tried it just to check up and see if it were possible, and it is very possible.

Judge Smith. You have made the matter perfectly clear. Is there anything more? I believe that what you were interested in knowing is now quite satisfactorily explained: that the deceased could have called the elevator from some other floor and had time to get back to the place where he was found dead.

John Riordan, a company representative, gave the final statement:

Q. You have no direct testimony to give?

A. No, only from observation.

Q. Then you will please give the vital statistics.

A. The name of the deceased is Claude M. Harvey, widower, born in Scotland on February 20, 1872. He has three children shown on the record, but from my knowledge, he has one daughter and two stepchildren. He was a boilermaker by trade, has worked for the United Verde Copper Company from 1914 to the present time. He was transferred from the 500 Shops on May 23, 1932, to position of fireman and engineer at the hospital.

Q. Has anybody any questions to ask this witness? Any further testimony you know of, Dr. Carlson?

Dr. Carlson. No.

Judge Smith. Then all those who are not members of the jury will be excused.

That was it. The coroner's jury brought in a verdict that Claude's death was accidental, adding, "The accident being unavoidable, we exonerate the company from all blame." The system being what it was at the time, no further investigating was done, and law enforcement did not get involved. But reading the transcript alone shows the weaknesses of asking common citizens to play detective, and this is why the system of coroner's juries has been largely abolished. Glaring questions arise from the testimony that would have been investigated in more depth today by qualified investigators, most notably John Zivkovich's truly bizarre statement that he saw Claude Harvey alive on an upper floor a scant three minutes before his head was crushed in the basement by a very slow-moving elevator.

Claude Harvey was buried in Greenwood Cemetery in Phoenix, next to his wife, Elizabeth, who had died six years earlier. Is his indeed one of the spirits that haunts Jerome Grand Hotel? If so, is this because the true story of his demise never came out?

Jerome Hogback Cemetery

Jerome's main town cemetery is located off the beaten track on a hill known as the Hogback. It is very old and has not received the best care over the years. The last recorded burial here occurred in 1919. The cemetery contains many unmarked graves.

Hogback Cemetery is a popular destination for ghost tours and paranormal investigators. Many have long reported that they obtained orb photographs and EVPs here. If you visit, please be respectful. Not everyone has treated the cemetery well over the years, and while it remains accessible, the town has been frustrated at times by careless visitors.

Lower Jerome Cemetery

Farther down the mountain on the Old Jerome Highway is the Lower Jerome Cemetery. This cemetery is adjacent to Clarkdale, and many have mistaken it as a Clarkdale cemetery. As the United Verde and UVX Mining Companies employed many Mexican immigrants as laborers, this is largely a Latino burial ground, where many mining men were interred.

If you visit, please be cautious. The cemetery is overgrown with scrub brush, and it is full of rocks and uneven trails. The place exudes an eerie atmosphere, especially in the evening. The growth of Clarkdale has seen a number of private homes sprout up near the cemetery's boundaries.

OATMAN

The small town of Oatman is located in the Black Mountains of Mohave County, along old Route 66, and is one of the towns along that highway that was bypassed by freeway access. Mining began here in the 1860s, when a prospector named John Moss began filing claims. He named one of his mining claims after Olive Oatman, a young girl whose story was well known. She had been kidnapped by Natives a decade earlier and was eventually released with her face tattooed. As a town started slowly growing in the area, it retained the name Oatman.

But mining prosperity did not come to Oatman until the twentieth century, when the United Eastern Mining Company struck a large gold deposit in 1915.

Tom Reed Gold
Mine in Oatman.
Nancy Burgess.

Also, the opening of the Tom Reed Mine brought added mining to the town. These events caused one of the last genuine gold rush booms in America. But in 1921, United Eastern shut down its operations, and in 1941, after the start of World War II, the federal government ordered all mining that was not benefitting the war effort to cease in America. After being bypassed by the major highways in the ensuing years, Oatman became all but a ghost town.

By the 1970s, Oatman had slowly begun reinventing itself as a tourist destination, especially in the wake of growing nostalgia for old Route 66. Oatman's population began growing again, and today, its economy is based almost completely on tourism. One of the draws is the area's wild burro population, which come into town and wander the streets most days. The burros are generally friendly, because they know the humans will feed them. The residents of Oatman have mixed feelings on this. Some shops sell bags of treats to give to the burros, while others wish people would stop feeding them so they will go away.

Oatman received some unwanted national attention in 1995, when Steven Colbern, a fugitive wanted by federal authorities as a person of interest in the bombing of the Alfred B. Murrah building in Oklahoma City, was arrested here.

Several old buildings in Oatman are reputedly haunted, most notably the old Oatman Hotel. Although it is no longer operated as a hotel, the owners have a room decorated and named for Hollywood performers Clark Gable and Carole Lombard, who, legend contends, spent their honeymoon here in 1939. This legend is very much in dispute, as some Hollywood historians say that Gable and Lombard never set foot in Oatman. Nevertheless, others have reported seeing their spirits roaming around the hotel building.

Left: The burros in Oatman run wild. *Darlene Wilson.*

Below: Oatman Hotel, Restaurant and Saloon. *Darlene Wilson.*

Old mining ruins outside of Oatman. *Darlene Wilson.*

The Oatman Hotel is reputed to be very eerie. Among other things, the ghost of an Irishman known as "Oatie" has been observed removing bedclothes from mattresses and opening the window of his former room. Oatie was a miner who resided in the hotel while working the nearby claims; according to the legend, one night, he drank too much and passed out behind the hotel, where his body was later discovered.

The ghost of a former chambermaid is thought to leave footprints of a prostrate corpse in the dust on the floor of a room on the second story. And throughout time, bartenders have also reported other disturbances. The lights have been left on, and the cash tips and glasses have levitated off the bar.

Witnesses have reported hearing eerie disembodied voices and seeing lights turn on and off by themselves, toilets flush in empty restrooms and footprints appear on freshly mopped floors.

Despite no longer accepting guests, the Oatman Hotel continues to function as a museum, restaurant, gift shop and much more.

It is reported that at one of the mines, a ghost still lingers nearby. According to legend, a miner's ghost might be wandering the mine, looking for objects that are long gone.

Prescott

President Abraham Lincoln signed the Organic Act on February 20, 1863, creating the Arizona Territory from a section of land that had been ceded by Mexico to America by force at the end of the Mexican-American War (1846–48). This required the president to appoint a set of officials and send them west to set up a new territorial government for Arizona. Initially, he appointed Ohio congressman John Addison Gurley to be governor of the new territory, but he unexpectedly died of an appendicitis attack before the party set out. On the recommendation of Richard McCormick, President Lincoln appointed former Maine congressman John Noble Goodwin to the post. McCormick was appointed secretary of the territory.

The first governor's party set out for its destination, traveling overland by coach—a long and arduous journey indeed. The party members were informally expected to set up the new capitol in Tucson, an old Mexican pueblo that was the only real town of any size in the new Arizona Territory. After crossing over into Arizona in December 1863, Governor Goodwin was informed by General James H. Carleton that Tucson was believed to be a hotbed of Confederate sympathizers (the Civil War was still going on at this time) and that this could make it a difficult place for a new Yankee government to set up shop. The Confederacy had already made a failed attempt to claim Arizona for itself.

The party stopped at Fort Whipple (then located at Del Rio Springs, which is somewhat north of Chino Valley) to get its bearings and decide what to do next. After much scouting and debating, the party traveled farther south of Fort Whipple and camped on the banks of Granite Creek. This area was inhabited by only a few stray miners and settlers, but the Arizona Territorial officials decided this was the place to establish Arizona's first capital. They christened the new town Prescott, named for the famed Boston-based historian William Hickling Prescott, who had died five years earlier. Naming a new town in honor of a man who had never set foot near the area was likely reflective of the New England dominance of the members of the governor' party; throughout the East Coast, William H. Prescott was held in high regard at this time.

Prescott was not destined to remain the capital, but the town remained and prospered. Its main source of industry and economic growth was mining. Gold and copper were the main ore deposits in the area, and in the ensuing decades, many small mining companies were formed in the Prescott area, as well as wildcat claims filed by individual miners.

The original 1864 Territorial Governor's Mansion in Prescott. It is now an integral part of the Sharlot Hall Museum. Recent paranormal investigations by Darlene Wilson have turned up quite a bit of ghostly activity. *Darlene Wilson.*

The Arizona Territory was finally granted statehood in 1912, becoming the forty-eighth state. But mining started to die out in the 1930s throughout Arizona, and Prescott was no exception.

Today, Prescott is a thriving metropolitan city with a population of over fifty thousand, not counting the neighboring cities of Prescott Valley and Chino Valley, which are almost as large. The growth of Prescott and its surrounding areas—most notable within the last thirty years—has been remarkable, with the population nearly quadrupling. Prescott is largely a retirement community today, with an economy based almost entirely on land development and tourism.

In 2018, this book's authors, Parker Anderson and Darlene Wilson, wrote the book *Haunted Prescott* for The History Press. Since that time, there have been new paranormal sightings and happenings at some of the locations listed in that book.

'Tis Art Center and Gallery

This historic structure was built in 1892 and is known as the Knights of Pythias building. Located in the heart of downtown Prescott, this building sat empty for twenty years before it was purchased and renovated. It is now home to 'Tis Art Center and Gallery, a nonprofit agency devoted to providing art education for children and adults and promoting local area artists (www.TisArtGallery.com).

Wilson and her friends Sandy and Lisa have often investigated this beautiful old building. During one investigation, they were joined by their friend Maureen. Patti of the 'Tis Art Gallery joined them as well, and they heard a dog in their recordings of the session. The following is a transcript from part of the investigation: Lisa is on the headphones, and they are doing an Estes session (see the appendix for a description of this equipment). The investigators asked questions, and Sandy transcribed the recording.

> *Q. Missed what?*
> *A. John. Mike.*
> *Q. Who is turning on the flashlight?*
> *A. It's the dog.*
> *Q. The dog is turning on the flashlight?*
> *A. Mike. Come here Mike. Mike!*
> *Q. Is the dog's name Mike?*
> *A. It's the dog. Come on. Mike*
> *Investigators. Don't hit it.*
> *A. We won't hit the dog, we love dogs!*
> [Lisa hears a dog barking.]
> *Q. Whose dog is this?*
> [There was no response, so the session was ended.]

Patti told the investigators about Mike, the community dog. None of them were aware of him, and they were so glad Patti was there to share her knowledge. She said Mike lived in the plaza and never belonged to anyone. The residents of Prescott tried to get Mike to go home with them, but Mike's home was in the plaza, greeting the people. People in town would go to dinner and order two steaks—one for themselves and one for Mike. She told the investigators there was a plaque in the plaza that was placed in Mike's honor. Later that day, the investigators found the plaque, and it was another connection, or validation, of what the spirit said during the Estes session.

On another investigation, Sandy set up her GoPro to see if it would record anything—and it did. It is one of the group's best recordings. They didn't see anything, but they did hear something. They heard a woman breathlessly say, "And next on stage are two of my favorites." The investigators believe she was an emcee for the Knights of Pythias parties, and they had many.

Prescott Center for the Arts

Once the Sacred Heart Church, the building was constructed in 1894, but by 1969 they outgrew the building and constructed a new, larger one several blocks away. This building was purchased by a woman who donated it to the Prescott Fine Arts Association and is now Suze's Prescott Center for the Arts.

In *Haunted Prescott*, Anderson and Wilson shared the building's history and a few of its haunted stories. Since that book's publication, Wilson and her friends Sandy and Lisa have investigated the area that is the Prescott Center's stage, but previously, it was where the Sacred Heart Church held mass.

When the investigators walked into the area, Wilson knew there were many spirits pacing back and forth. She knew there were some that wanted to "cross over," so she said, "Those that want help in crossing over, line up on my right." When the investigators went through the photographs from their investigation, the first picture showed a room full of orbs—dozens of them. It was the same in the second picture, and the third picture showed all the orbs lined up on Wilson's right.

Palace Saloon and Restaurant

The Palace Saloon is the oldest saloon in Arizona, the oldest business on Whiskey Row and the most actively haunted place in Prescott. The authors of this book tell stories of the saloon's history and ghost stories in *Haunted Prescott*, but there are many more stories to tell.

Wilson has done many investigations in the Palace Saloon and has performed several energy clearings there to get rid of negative energy. She gets called in when things get out of control; for example: when sixty-pound stage pieces levitate and land on a customer, the paper towel dispenser in the ladies' restroom flies off the wall and hits a customer or when the thick saloon glasses just shatter on the table, some empty and some with drinks in them. When Wilson goes in and does a clearing, everything settles down—for a while.

One evening, Stacy, an employee of the Palace Saloon, was closing and vacuuming the floors when she rounded the corner where the restrooms are and saw a man standing there. She noticed his black boots first, then his black jeans and shirt, the soot on his face and huge eyes, shocked to have been seen. Then she watched him morph into the wall of the ladies' restroom. She touched the wall to see if it was cold or hot—it was hot.

A week later, a group of kids came in for lunch. One called over Emma, the general manager, and asked her about the man standing by the restrooms. Emma asked him what the man looked like, and he said, "Black boots, black jeans, black shirt and a dirty face."

A few days later, a mother and her six-year-old daughter came in for lunch. The little girl asked Emma about the man standing by the restrooms. She described the same man.

Wilson was called in to do a clearing in the ladies' restroom. There is a window on one wall that faces a huge mirror on the other wall, making it a portal and easy for an entity to enter the space. With the right setup—a mirror opposite from a window for example—a portal opens like a vent, allowing spirits to come through. These may be good or bad spirits.

Wilson did the clearing in the restroom, and she put up a nice curtain, but behind the curtain, she also hung a crystal. So, when an entity tries to enter, the crystal will disperse its energy, blocking it from entering the space. At the time of this writing, the clearing took place five months ago, and it seems to be working well.

STANTON

In the southern portion of Yavapai County, below Yarnell Hill, lies a remote section of desert that was once the Weaver Mining District. Central to this area was Rich Hill, which is still visible for miles around and is identifiable by a long streak down its center. Rich Hill is so named because in 1863, a prospecting party led by pioneer Abraham Peeples discovered the richest gold strike in Arizona there. This strike is perhaps second only to the Vulture Mine near Wickenburg. Unverified legend contends the Peeples party actually found large gold nuggets just lying on the ground there.

As word of this strike spread, wildcat ore and placer miners descended on the Rich Hill area in droves, and the newly formed Weaver Mining District (named for early Arizona explorer Pauline Weaver) became one of the busiest mining areas in the Arizona Territory, with scores of mining claims being filed.

As with all mining districts of the era, in Weaver Mining District, towns sprouted up to serve the miners' needs. Three towns appeared in the shadow of Rich Hill and were named Weaver, Octave and Antelope Station (or just Antelope), the last one being the primary stagecoach stop between the larger towns of Wickenburg and Prescott.

Small mining towns like these consisted of cabins for the miners and mercantile stores where they could get supplies, as well as eating establishments and, of course, saloons. Every mining town had to have saloons, as the miners (after a hard day or week of work) usually wanted to go out and celebrate their good fortunes or drink away their bad fortunes. Contrary to popular belief, little towns like these did not have active red-light districts where prostitution was practiced. Women were scarce in areas such as these, and the men had to travel to larger towns by stagecoach whenever they wanted female comforts.

The Weaver Mining District and its three towns were so remote that the area became attractive to outlaws, bandits and other miscreants who were hiding out from the law. As more of them moved to Weaver, Octave and Antelope, the area developed a reputation for being unsafe. It became an area where a lot of crime was occurring and not much in the way of law enforcement was present. The area officially had a constable and a justice of the peace, but they were inadequate to maintain law and order in an area as rough as the Weaver District.

The Legend of Charles P. Stanton

In the early 1870s, a man of mystery named Charles P. Stanton moved to Antelope. He was an Irish immigrant who spoke with a brogue and also spoke fluent Spanish. Little is known of his background, and he is not known to have volunteered much information about his life (although he did once claim to have fled the United Kingdom due to political persecution). Stanton purchased some mining claims and laid claim to others on his own.

His claim on the Leviathan Mine made him a very rich man, and he opened a mercantile store in Antelope. Recognizing the area's bad reputation, he set to work to boost the town into something better. He was elected justice of the peace and persuaded the U.S. government to establish a post office in Antelope. For this, he was rewarded with the appointment of postmaster, and in filling out the official paperwork, he renamed the town for himself. The mining town of Antelope became Stanton, Arizona. Stanton himself was nicknamed the "Irish Lord" in his own lifetime.

Much folklore exists about Charles P. Stanton. It has been handed down through the generations and is largely accepted as fact by most Arizona historians. Legend asserts that Stanton quickly became the town "boss" in Antelope and was responsible for countless murders, robberies and other depredations in this crime-ridden area. Legends further state that the miners in the Weaver District lived in mortal terror of him and that he escaped arrest and prosecution because he had the Yavapai County law enforcement officials bought and paid for.

The legend of Stanton continues to be told and accepted as fact today. But in his book *Arizona Gold Gangster Charles P. Stanton: Truth and Legend in Yavapai's Dark Days* (The History Press, 2020), historian Parker Anderson casts doubt on the veracity of many of these tales by researching old court papers, county records and newspapers. A thorough study of these reveals many documented contradictions with the legends.

The legend of Charles P. Stanton as evil incarnate originated in Stanton's lifetime, with prominent area pioneer and miner Charles Genung somehow convinced that Stanton was responsible for every depredation being committed in the crime-infested Weaver Mining District. Genung tried in vain for years to get law enforcement officials to go after Stanton, but without evidence more solid than Genung's word, they did not do so.

One of the best-known murders that occurred in territorial Yavapai County occurred in Antelope in 1877, when resident William Partridge shot and killed stage stop proprietor George M. "Yaqui" Wilson. Partridge pleaded he killed Wilson in self-defense, claiming in court that Wilson (with whom he was already on bad terms) assaulted him with a sledgehammer handle. After Partridge managed to reach his gun, he shot Wilson in the heat of the moment. Partridge was convicted of second-degree murder and sentenced to ten years at Yuma Territorial Prison, but he was paroled after only two years and returned to Antelope, where he managed to resume his life.

Legend and folklore, feeding off the later statements of Charles Genung, tell a wildly different story. The traditional story, told around campfires for generations, is that Charles P. Stanton tricked Partridge into killing George M. Wilson. According to this legend, Stanton sent word to Partridge that Wilson was gunning for him, knowing that Partridge would fly into a panic, run downtown (wherever downtown was) and shoot Wilson on sight. Stanton's alleged motive? To get Wilson out of the way so he could grab the stage stop business. This scenario sounds like bad melodrama, but thanks to its endorsement by Genung, it has had a lengthy lifespan. But as noted previously, Partridge's surviving court papers tell a much different story.

George M. "Yaqui" Wilson's partner in the stage stop business was a man named John Timmerman. Two years later, in 1879, Timmerman was ambushed and murdered on the road between Antelope and Wickenburg. Robbery was apparently the motive, as a large amount of money he had been carrying was missing. Of course, today's folklore contends that Stanton had his hired assassins (a Mexican gang) kill Timmerman so he could grab the stage stop.

In actuality, soon after John Timmerman's murder, Stanton was arrested on a minor theft charge for allegedly stealing a gold nugget. This was apparently part of a sting operation, as while he was in jail, the sheriff's office (undoubtedly goaded on by Genung) desperately tried to find evidence tying the Irish Lord to Timmerman's tragic demise. They did not find anything. Stanton was later released from jail, the theft charge dismissed on a technicality.

But was Stanton responsible for Timmerman's murder? Legend and folklore continue to say he was, but a search of Yavapai County property records show that before his passing, John Timmerman had sold the stage stop. This revelation takes away the motive for murder that legend has given Stanton. In an area this small and remote, a new proprietor of the stage stop would have been well known to residents.

Other residents of the town of Stanton were Barney Martin and his strong-willed wife, Rosa, who operated what would today be called a "bed-and-breakfast" establishment. The Martins had two children, John and William (they were likely Barney's children, and Rosa was their stepmother). After a tumultuous six years in town, the Martins had packed up and were apparently moving away. On the road to Phoenix, the family was ambushed by bandits and massacred near the town of Wittman.

The Martin massacre was never officially solved; the killers were never caught, and the case remains on the list of worst crimes ever committed in Arizona. Charles Genung once again tried to convince law enforcement officials that Charles P. Stanton was responsible but was unable to provide evidence of this. However, legend and folklore continue to attribute this ghastly crime to him, going so far as to add an unsubstantiated story that Stanton stood on a nearby hill, laughing maniacally as his henchmen slaughtered the family. So, who saw him and recorded this? Legends never stop to consider basic questions like this.

A few months after the Martin killings, Charles P. Stanton was himself shot and killed in his store by three Mexican gunmen on the night of November 13, 1886. The traditional Stanton legend contends that Stanton had propositioned the sister of the men, and they killed him for revenge. But Charles Genung liked to hint that he had orchestrated the hit on Stanton, and under the circumstances, it is easy to believe he did.

The lawlessness of the Weaver Mining District and the towns of Stanton, Octave and Weaver did not end with Stanton's death, and on November 30, 1898, the Prescott newspaper *Arizona Journal Miner* called for the entire area to be wiped out and obliterated from the map due to the continuing crimes being committed there. But ultimately, the mining began dying out in the early twentieth century, and by the 1930s, the once prominent towns

The renovated Hotel Stanton in Stanton, Arizona. The ghost town where much violence once occurred is now an RV park for the Lost Dutchman Mining Association. *Parker Anderson.*

of Stanton, Octave and Weaver were mostly ghost towns. Today, nothing is left of Weaver and Octave except for a few foundations and the now-derelict town cemeteries.

The town of Stanton, however, had some of its original buildings still standing in the 1970s, when the site was purchased by the Lost Dutchman Mining Association (LDMA). The company renovated the old buildings and got the remote area hooked up for electricity and water. Stanton is now used as an RV park for LDMA's members during mining season, when they are working their placer and ore claims each year.

A town with a bloody history like Stanton's is bound to have its share of hauntings.

Residents of the LDMA RV Park reportedly see shadows lurking around the buildings at night. There have been reports of a ghostly woman dressed in a bridal gown peering out of the second-story window of the old Stanton Hotel. This ghost town turned RV park has also become a destination for paranormal investigators during the off-season, when there aren't as many residents and miners around.

YARNELL

Highway 89 continues from Congress up a steep, winding hill known as Yarnell Hill. In the early 1970s, the road was turned into a divided highway to ease traffic congestion on the narrow road (again, this was before Interstate 17 bypassed this entire area going from Phoenix to Prescott and beyond).

The small town of Yarnell, at the top of the hill, was a mining town in its earliest days, as small wildcat miners struck claims in the area. Pioneer Charles Genung is believed to have been the first of these miners, striking gold in the area in 1865. The town is named for Harrison Yarnell, a prospector about whom little is known, although he died in 1916 and was buried in Mountain View Cemetery in Prescott.

Before I-17 became the main route from Phoenix going north, Yarnell (and the neighboring town in Peeples Valley) was a pleasant rest stop for motorists on the road, with motels and restaurants along the main street. These are mostly gone now, and Yarnell is now a largely quiet retirement community with a population of around seven hundred.

Granite Mountain Hotshots

A major tragedy occurred in the community in the hot summer of 2013. A major wildfire, known as the Yarnell Hill Fire, broke out in the mountains surrounding Yarnell and Peeples Valley. The entire area was evacuated, and many homes were destroyed. A special firefighting unit of twenty men from Prescott known as the Granite Mountain Hotshots was dispatched to help fight the out-of-control blaze.

On June 30, 2013, nineteen of the hotshots died in the fire almost simultaneously when the flames suddenly raged down on them on the mountain. There was one survivor. The tragedy made national news, and a number of landmarks have been renamed in their honor. The area where they died has been turned into a somber state park with a long hiking trail beginning on Yarnell Hill.

Shrine of St. Joseph of the Mountains

Yarnell's most prominent tourist attraction is the Shrine of St. Joseph, a Roman Catholic shrine built on the side of a boulder-covered mountain. Through a winding and often steep trail, visitors pass by stark white statues and wooden crosses, representing the stations of the cross and the final hours of the life of Jesus Christ on Earth.

The shrine was formed in the 1930s by the Phoenix-based Catholic Action League, founded by William Wasson and his wife, Mary. Wasson owned land in Yarnell and thought it would be an appropriate location for a shrine, so the Catholic Action League commissioned a statue of St. Joseph holding the child Jesus from a Phoenix sculptor, and the shrine opened in 1939.

The Wassons wanted to expand the shrine with trails and more statues, and they went searching for a sculptor. They hired an itinerant, sometimes homeless artist named Felix Lucero, who had been creating religious art in Tucson, some of which is still standing in that city. The Wassons were inspired by Lucero's story. During World War I, he was critically wounded on the battlefield, and in what he believed were his dying moments, he promised the Virgin Mary that if he were spared, he would devote the remainder of his life to creating Catholic art and statues of Jesus. Lucero was rescued, and he survived, so he made good on his promise to the Virgin Mary and began creating statues out of any material he could find.

The entrance sign to the famous Shrine of St. Joseph of the Mountains in Yarnell, Arizona. *Darlene Wilson.*

One of the statues in the Shrine of St. Joseph depicts Jesus in torment in the Garden of Gethsemane. *Darlene Wilson.*

After being hired by the Wassons, he created six statues: a new St. Joseph, Jesus at the Last Supper, Jesus in the Garden of Gethsemane, the crucifixion, Mary cradling the body of Jesus and Jesus lying in his tomb. The job took him the rest of the decade, and the sculptures were completed by 1949. There have been reports that Lucero was to have sculpted the apostles at the Last Supper as well (Jesus is sitting alone at the table at the Shrine), but he died of injuries suffered in a house fire shortly after completing his main body of work.

The shrine is still owned and operated by the Wasson family. In later years, they added a retreat center, gift shop and restrooms and commissioned a new bronze statue of the risen Christ.

But in 2013, as the Yarnell Hill Fire rained down on the town, the Wasson family had to evacuate with the rest of the area's populace. The fire raged through the shrine. When the family was allowed to return over a week later, they discovered the buildings—the gift shop and retreat center—were total losses, but the statues and wooden crosses were miraculously unharmed. There were burned and charred trees and bushes just inches away from them, but they sustained little or no damage (with the exception of the cross at the crucifixion scene, part of which burned away at the top, but the statue was untouched). The Wassons' home was also untouched. Yarnell residents believed the survival of the shrine from the devastating fire was a genuine miracle from God.

The Shrine of St. Joseph can be visited daily in Yarnell, although you need good physical stamina to hike the entire trail. Visitors feel inspired here. They often feel they are not alone and come away believing there is indeed something very holy about this little place of worship.

Carraro's Grotto

Down the road from the shrine are the ruins of a former tourist attraction in Yarnell that was known as Carraro's Grotto. The ruins are now located on private property and cannot be visited without permission, although the front can be seen from the road.

Alessio Carraro was a visionary architect and businessman who designed the famous Tovrea Castle in Phoenix. But in his later years, he retired to Yarnell, where he had purchased a boulder-covered lot on Shrine Road. There, he foresaw a possible tourist attraction, and he spent a number of years forging trails between the large boulders and painting signs on

Alessio Carraro's "Zoo of Rocks" Grotto in Yarnell in its prime. Today, the former tourist attraction is in ruins. *Sharlot Hall Museum.*

some boulders with the names of animals and other things he thought the individual boulders resembled.

Carraro christened the site as the Zoo of Rocks Grotto, and it appeared in promotions for Yarnell and on postcards. He constructed a small cabin at the top of the grotto, where he slept at night, and by day, he resided in a small trailer at the base of the grotto. Author Parker Anderson's grandparents lived in Yarnell during this period, and they told him he slept up in the cabin so he could be closer to God at night.

It was a unique site in its day, but upon Carraro's death in 1964, the grotto sat alone, vacant and largely uncared for. Visitors still came, and author Anderson often played there as a child. But the years eventually took their toll, and Carraro's Grotto is now a ruin, with many of Carraro's painted signs having faded in the sun, though some are still extant.

Southwest Arizona

Ajo

The town of Ajo was once one of the major copper mining hubs of the American Southwest. Although there was reportedly some mining activity as early as the late 1850s (before Arizona was even declared a territory), profitable mining in Ajo did not start in earnest until the 1890s.

At that time, two partners, A.J. Shotwell and John Boddie, organized the St. Louis Copper Company, which they later renamed the New Cornelia after Boddie's wife. Mining went slowly but adequately for nearly twenty years. Then in 1911, John Campbell Greenway came into the picture.

Greenway studied engineering at Yale University, where he was also a star athlete. He also served as one of Theodore Roosevelt's Rough Riders during the 1898 Spanish-American War. Following the war, he went to work for U.S. Steel and was sent to the Arizona Territory to help manage copper mines in Bisbee, which were owned by the Calumet Company.

Reportedly, after seeing ore samples from the Cornelia Mine at Ajo, Greenway visited the site, where he persuaded Boddie to sell the New Cornelia to Calumet. Following the sale, Greenway stepped up efforts in copper mining in the difficult area, and in 1916, he patented a new, successful method of leaching copper ore.

By 1917, the New Cornelia was a million-dollar operation, using steam shovels, conveyor belts and around-the-clock operations. The town of

The town of Ajo in the 1920s. *Nancy Burgess.*

Ajo was growing because of this, and the town had a booming economy. Greenway resigned as the manager in 1925.

During World War I, Greenway entered the military and fought in France. He became a brigadier general in the U.S. Army Reserve. He resigned as manager of the New Cornelia in 1925.

John Campbell Greenway died on January 19, 1926, following gallbladder surgery. His funeral in Ajo was attended by over three thousand people. Because of Greenway's influence in the state, Arizona commissioned a large statue of him (by sculptor Gutzon Borglum of Mount Rushmore fame) to be placed in Statuary Hall in the U.S. Capitol in Washington, D.C., where every state can have two statues representing its major historical leaders. Greenway's widow, Isabella, later ran successfully for Congress, becoming the first woman to serve in the U.S. House of Representatives from Arizona. She served from 1933 to 1937.

But times change, and as the decades passed, Arizona started to forget what a giant John Campbell Greenway had been in Arizona. First, at the request of his family members, in 1995, Greenway's body was disinterred and reburied in his wife's family plot in Kentucky. This went virtually unnoticed by the media and the state so many decades after Greenway's burial in Ajo.

Second, in 2015, Arizona removed Greenway's statue from Statuary Hall in Washington, D.C., and replaced it with a large statue of Arizona senator (and 1964 presidential candidate) Barry Goldwater. Borglum's statue of Greenway is now on display at the Arizona State Library and Archives in Phoenix.

As for mining in Ajo, it continued. In 1931, the Calumet Company merged with Phelps Dodge, then and now one of the largest copper mining corporations in America. Mining continued over the decades, with Ajo

The haunted and abandoned Phelps Dodge Hospital. *Tony Rathman.*

being pretty much a typical mining town. This continued until 1983, when the miners' unions, led by United Steelworkers, went on strike against Phelps Dodge in Ajo, Morenci and Douglas.

The three-year strike is now remembered as a key event in the history of organized labor in the United States. It was marked with mass protests, large picket lines and outbreaks of violence against mining officials and strike-breaking workers. Buoyed by President Ronald Reagan's war on the labor unions in America, Phelps Dodge dug in its heels and began hiring nonunion labor, with the strike breakers reporting for work amid threats and incidents of extreme violence.

Because of all this, copper prices plummeted drastically, and Phelps Dodge closed the Ajo mines in 1985. The town of Ajo went into an economic depression, one from which it has never fully recovered. But the town has survived, and in recent years, it has reinvented itself as a retirement community. Many people who retire in Arizona now choose Ajo as their home for its balmy quiet and surrounding scenery.

Phelps Dodge Hospital

Hospitals can be some of the most haunted places in the world. Hospitals are full of people who are in pain and often dying. Some believe this energy can be stored in hospital walls. Many stories of hospital hauntings center on the spirits of the dead who cannot move on from this world and remain in the hospital, often in the room where they passed away. These spirits are said to appear in the hallways, rooms or morgues and may interact with the living.

Staff members, nurses and doctors who have a solid connection to the hospital may also linger after death. Not all hospital ghosts are dark; some may stay there, feeling they can help the ill. Other hauntings of hospitals include incidents of unexplained sounds, cold spots and objects moving independently.

Tony Rathman is the founder and lead investigator of Entity Voices. He and his wife, Cherie Rathman, a cofounder and investigator, have spent the last decade discovering the truths about spirits, entities and life after death. They were both part of the Copper Canyon Paranormal Research Center and had access to the Phelps Dodge Hospital in Ajo, Arizona. (Find more information about Entity Voices Paranormal Investigation at https://entityvoices.com/.)

The Phelps Dodge Hospital is a twenty-nine-thousand-square-foot abandoned hospital with a rich history of supporting injured miners and their families. Tony, Cherie and their team of investigators have spent a lot of time in this hospital. They have heard the cries of babies coming from the pediatrics section. They listen to the voices of ghosts answering the questions they ask, and it is all recorded using their equipment.

An abandoned hallway in Phelps Dodge Hospital. *Tony Rathman.*

Darlene Wilson has investigated the hospital with eleven other people. She spotted the ghost of an orderly, dressed all in white, standing at the end of the long hall—just standing there, staring at her. When she started walking toward him, he vanished.

At the end of the evening, five of the investigators, including Wilson, decided to sit in the hallway with their recording equipment, and they started asking questions. Suddenly, they heard someone walking around in the corner room on the first floor. The room had been the doctor's office and exam room. It sounded like crunching paper or possible dry paint chips falling from the ceilings. The investigators had also put down a large sheet of paper with baby powder on it to see if they could capture any ghostly footprints. They didn't, but they heard the crunch of footsteps in that room.

All of their meters kept going off in the nurse's station, their lights changing colors from green to red, indicating the presence of ghostly energy. One could feel the difference in energy in that entire area.

The investigators also recorded EVPs and Estes sessions in the hospital lobby and got a nurse from the pediatric ward to talk to them. A man demanded to see his wife and said the babies were upset and crying.

Vinnie Amico and his team from the AZ Paranormal Investigation and Research Society have also investigated the hospital. He said that at one point, he and his wife, Pamela, stood in front of a door and heard footsteps coming up behind them. The door handle started jiggling. Amico pushed down on the handle, the door swung open and they felt an eerie emptiness. (Find more information on the AZ Paranormal Investigation and Research Society at https://www.azpirs.com/.)

Others have shared their stories as well. One is that of a lost child who has been heard crying in one of the hospital rooms. Investigators believe it is the spirit of a child who passed away in the hospital and is now looking for his parents.

Another story is that of a woman in a gray dress who is seen walking through the halls of the hospital. Some believe her spirit began roaming the hospital after she passed away there before it closed.

The hospital is for sale as of 2023. The person who owns the building now does not allow paranormal investigations. Hopefully, the ghosts that are still lingering there will be pleased with whatever the future holds for this building.

CASTLE DOME CITY

The Castle Dome City is now a ghost town and a museum with fifty original buildings. It was settled around 1863 as a transport depot and mining camp in the Arizona Territory. It is located about forty miles north of Yuma, Arizona, in the Sonoran Desert and is surrounded by the majestic, rugged beauty of the Chihuahuan Desert. The landscape is dominated by rolling hills and large desert vistas with distant mountain ranges.

The road leading to Castle Dome is a rough dirt path that is graded and taken care of—it's just bumpy in places. Any vehicle can drive the road, just take it nice and slow. During monsoon season, this might be a different story. Call the museum and find out before venturing out there.

Along the Colorado River, various mining camps and steamboat ports developed into towns as new mineral resources were found along the river. Conner and Snively created the Castle Dome Mining Company in 1863.

Conflicts with Natives delayed the start of mining operations for several years. The first mining camps appeared around 1869. The town took on the name Castle Dome as the area grew, getting its first post office in 1875, but it lasted for just one year.

Steamboats on the Colorado River prospered when the mining camps went out of business, and the post office reopened in 1878 under the name Castle Dome Landing. As it did in many towns, the activity in Castle Dome dwindled, and in 1884, the post office closed. Because of the source of lead and the First and Second World Wars, the mines were reopened. In 1943, a

Castle Dome City, a ghost town. *Darlene Wilson.*

Castle Dome Landing's paddle wheel. It was once a small port that shipped supplies and ore. *Sharlot Hall Museum.*

different mining firm reopened to satisfy the demands of the war. By 1978, all the mines were closed, and the final residents left.

Castle Dome Landing's ruins are currently buried beneath the reservoir of the Imperial Dam. Allen and Stephanie Armstrong bought the land that once housed the mining camp and town of Castle Dome in 1994, and it is now the Castle Dome Museum. There are fifty restored buildings in the town, and seven of them are town-built originals from a century ago.

The new town has many of the artifacts that were discovered in the old town. The saloon, Carmelita's Cantina, has food cans from the 1800s, old

Castle Dome City Ghost Town Store. *Darlene Wilson.*

mining tables and the bar. The mercantile store is full of old food cans from the 1800s from the original Castle Dome location. The old carbide cans and powder boxes are also original.

Allen and Stephanie Armstrong, with permission, salvaged structures, relics and stacks of wood—whatever they could—from the old town site. They studied old newspapers and any historical documents they could find to rebuild the town. What you see today is the hard work of Allen and Stephanie and their many volunteers.

Since he was a young boy, Allen Armstrong dreamed of owning a place like Castle Dome. He and his wife, Stephanie, bought Castle Dome in 1993. Officials of the refuge said they would be clearing everything there, so Allen offered to take everything he could. It took him years to transport everything to the new location. He gathered buildings and reclaimed materials, going down shafts to collect old mining tools and supplies.

Prostitution was not illegal in Castle Dome in the 1800s and early 1900s. Prostitutes would travel to the mining camps to provide services for the miners. The prostitutes would set up makeshift brothels in the area and/ or work out of saloons, hotels and other establishments. The town had a reputation for being dangerous and unruly. The prostitutes were known to be very aggressive and sometimes violent in their dealings with customers. By the 1930s, prostitution in Castle Dome had primarily disappeared, as the town began to decline.

One madam, Toole Handley, started her brothel business in San Francisco. She and her girls would follow the miners, toting her brass bathtub from camp to camp. She would make the men take a bath before spending any time with her girls. She died in the 1920s at the age of ninety-three. Her tub is still there in Castle Dome.

Stories of the hauntings in and around Castle Dome can only be imagined. Just because the buildings were moved doesn't mean the ghosts of the miners don't still linger there.

In several stories Darlene Wilson heard about the ghosts of Castle Dome, according to local legend, a mysterious figure wearing a long black cloak and a wide-brimmed hat can often be seen roaming the area around Castle Dome Landing. The figure is said to appear at night, silently gliding through the shadows of the site, and seems to be searching for something. And then the figure disappears as quickly as it appears. Some claim to have seen the figure's face hidden in the darkness with a menacing stare and a sinister smile.

Locals claim to have seen a mysterious figure wandering around Castle Dome Landing. He is shrouded in a white mist and is believed to be the figure of a soldier who died during the Civil War and is searching for his lost love.

WICKENBURG

Following the end of the Mexican War in 1848 and then the Gadsden Purchase of 1853, much of the newly acquired land went unexplored and unused by the government. In the period before Arizona was declared an official territory in 1864, Arizona saw a few stray miners and settlers come into the area to see what they could find. Among them was a Prussian (some sources say German) immigrant named Henry Wickenburg. Very little is known of Wickenburg's background before he came to America.

Wickenburg located one of the very first major gold strikes in Arizona in 1864. He named his claim the Vulture for reasons that are unknown, but they have been often speculated on. From that time to the present day, the Vulture Mine has yielded more than $30 million in gold. A large mountain overlooking the mine has been named Vulture Peak.

Rich mining claims in those days usually caused towns to sprout up around them, housing and servicing the miners in those operations. The Vulture Mine was so large and rich that two towns sprouted up nearby. They were Vulture City, located near the mine site itself (now a ghost town), and,

Top: Wickenburg in the 1930s. *Nancy Burgess.*

Bottom: Vulture Gold Mine outside of Wickenburg, Arizona. *Nancy Burgess.*

later, the town of Wickenburg (named for its founder, Henry Wickenburg), which was located some miles away.

Henry Wickenburg was deeded 160 acres of land in 1879 by President Rutherford Hayes under a government program, and he began parceling out lots for sale in the town that would bear his name. In his lifetime, he became a member of the seventh territorial legislature and served as postmaster, justice of the peace and in a number of other positions in the town of Wickenburg. But he had already sold his claim to the Vulture to a group of New York investors by late 1865 for $25,000. It was a move he would later regret, as the newly formed New York–based Vulture Mining Company began churning out untold wealth in gold.

By the early twentieth century, Henry Wickenburg was very old and needed a caretaker, who was named Hellene Holland. He was found dead of a gunshot wound on May 14, 1905; his death was ruled a suicide by a local coroner's inquest. He was eighty-five years old and had been living on a very modest income since his unfortunate decision to sell the Vulture Mine. Some Wickenburg historians today doubt that he died by suicide and believe he was perhaps murdered by his caretaker, Hellene Holland, and her husband, William, so they could get their hands on his money and belongings.

Some reports have said the Hollands were, or claimed to be, Spiritualists, and used this to influence Henry's financial decisions (to their benefit) through communications from the spirit world.

Today, Henry Wickenburg's home and grave site are local historic sites that may be toured by visitors. The tiny cemetery where Wickenburg was buried was neglected for many years but has recently been spruced up and cared for by local residents.

Wickenburg Massacre

In the early days of the Arizona Territory, settlers and miners were often beset by Native attacks as the various tribes in the area sought to drive the white men from their land. The town of Wickenburg was no exception.

On November 5, 1871, one of the best known of these incidents occurred. About six miles outside of town, a stagecoach was attacked, and six men were brutally slain. Among them was Boston journalist Frederick Loring, who was on assignment in the territory. Two passengers, identified as William Kruger and Mollie Sheppard (the only female on the stage), apparently escaped. Kruger later said that Mollie Sheppard died of her wounds at a much later date, but this is unconfirmed; her fate is officially unknown.

Kruger penned the following letter addressed to William G. Peckham in New York City, detailing his version of what happened, and it was published in many newspapers across America as news of the atrocity spread.

Dear Sir: In acknowledging the receipt of your letter of November 16, 1871, I am pleased to be able to give you an account of the death of my friend [Frederick] *Loring, who was well-known to me and whose untimely death is deeply regretted by me. We left Fort Whipple, near Prescott, Arizona Territory, on Saturday, November 4, in the best of health and spirit. To be sure, the stage was rather crowded, but being all of such good temper, we had a real nice time. Loring being the most lively of us all, anticipating a speedy return to his friends East. Well, he retained his inside seat until we reached Wickenburg, on Sunday morning, November 5, 1871, when, after leaving there, he preferred to have an outside seat, to* which I most decidedly objected; but he insisted on being outside for a short time. I had two revolvers and he had none; in fact, no arms whatever. He rejected my offer of a revolver, saying at the time, "My dear Kruger, we are now comparatively safe. I have traveled with Lieutenant Wheeler for nearly eight months, and have never seen an Indian." Well, we rolled on until about 11:00 A.M., when the fatal attack was made.

The first warning I had was the warning cry of the driver, who cried "Apaches! Apaches!" At the same moment the Indians, who lay concealed, fired the first volley, killing poor Loring, the driver, and the other outside passenger, a Mr. Adams. They killed also the off-lead horse and wounded the other lead horse. The horses, very much frightened, then ran forward about twenty yards, when they came to a sudden stop. At the same time Loring fell off the stage and so did the other passenger. At the same moment the Indians fired the second volley from three sides—the both sides and rear—not more than four or five yards from the stage, killing Mr. Shoholm, one of the inside passengers, and wounding Miss Shephard [sic], myself, and a Mr. Salmon, of Lieutenant Wheeler's party. The latter one was mortally wounded and fell out of the stage, and crawled away, but was finally captured by the Indians, scalped and otherwise mutilated. The only one not then wounded was Mr. Hammet, of Lieutenant Wheeler's party. Both he and myself commenced immediately firing. Both fired six shots. Not having any more ammunition, I ceased firing. The Indians then disappeared behind the bushes.

But what a terrible spectacle it was to see the six dead bodies in plain sight! Loring was lying right under my very eyes, not yet dead, but suffering, apparently, terribly. He was shot through the left temple, his right eye and his lungs. He suffered for about four minutes, but I was positive that he died before I made my escape. Knowing that it would be useless to attempt to escape until the Indians would come back to plunder the stage, I remained perfectly quiet, having in the meantime ascertained that Miss Shephard was yet alive, but badly wounded. She succeeded in getting a loaded revolver from one of the killed passengers, which she gave to me. I then told her to keep cool and to be ready to run as soon as I would give the signal. Well, in about six minutes of terrible suspense I saw the Indians slowly creeping towards the stage. I counted and saw plainly fifteen Indians all dressed in blue soldiers' trousers. When they came within five yards of the stage, I jumped up, yelled and fired at them.

The woman, at the same time, yelled also, and we succeeded admirably in driving them off for the time being and got time to leave the stage. Before

I left the stage I cried out as loud as I possibly could if anyone was left alive, but only Mr. Adams answered, but was mortally wounded and could not even move his hands or feet, so I had to leave him to his fate. He was afterward found with his throat cut and otherwise mutilated. The Indians afterward followed me for about five miles, and I had a running fight with them until I fell in with the "buckboard." I had to carry the wounded woman for over two miles on my left arm. I myself received one shot through the right arm-pit, coming out on the shoulder, and two shots in my back. The woman also had three shots, one dangerous.

How I could escape with my life, and be able to save the life of Miss Shephard, is more than I can account for. That I left my mark with the Indians, there is no doubt, because two Indians died from gun-shot wounds at Camp Date Creek Reservation; but the commanding officer refused to have the thing investigated, for fear he would find sufficient evidence that they were his pets—that is, Camp Date Creek Indians. At all events, there is no doubt whatever that the outrage was committed by Indians and by the Camp Date Creek Indians, those so-called friendly Indians who Uncle Sam feeds!

After the news reached Wickenburg, we were brought to Wickenburg after sixteen hours of terrible suffering and agony. I stopped at the place of attack and closed the eyes of all my poor traveling companions. Loring, poor boy, was not mutilated, but looked calm and peaceful, excepting his fearful wound through the head. He wore "soldiers' clothing." His hat is in my possession now; if you wish it you can have it. Loring and four of his companions in fate were decently buried the next day, Monday, November 8, 1871, in nice coffins. I saw them buried. The other man who got scalped was buried on the road. Mr. [Thomas] Sexton, of the Vulture Mine at Wickenburg, attended to the funeral. Rest assured that our friend Loring had a decent funeral. Peace be with his ashes. I forwarded everything belonging to Loring to Lieutenant Wheeler, excepting his hat, which you can have should you desire it. There are four bullet-holes through the same. What Loring lost I don't profess to know. I know I lost everything but my life. The Indians got, to my certain knowledge, about twenty-five thousand dollars—nine thousand dollars belonging to me and Miss Shephard.

There is not a particle of doubt in my mind that the attacking party were Indians. I have known Indians since the last five years, and cannot be mistaken; besides, all indications show that they were Indians. Every citizen here will swear to it, because those citizens tracked the Indians from place of outrage to Camp Date Creek. But the commanding officer,

Captain [Richard F.] *O'Beirne, Twenty-first Infantry, not only allowed the Indians to go unpunished, but also refused me, Miss Shephard, the two surviving cripples, shelter. Yes, Sir, he ordered us off his reservation, and I wish to heaven you would publish this act of inhumanity in your New York papers. Please show this letter to Mr. Loring* [father of the deceased], *Boston, Massachusetts, who wrote to me the same time you did.*
I am, Sir, very truly yours,
William Kruger
Chief Clerk to Captain C.W. Foster, A.S.M.
United States Army, Ehrenburg, Arizona Territory

Authorities at the time blamed the incident, which came to be known as the Wickenburg Massacre, on the Yavapai Indian tribe (often erroneously believed to be the Apache tribe at that time), largely due to Kruger's testimony. General George Crook, then in command of military operations against Natives in the territory, believed he had traced the killers to a Native encampment at Burro Creek, under the command of Chief Ochocama, and sent a detachment to arrest them. A fierce battle ensued, in which many died.

In the ensuing years, the identity of the perpetrators was in dispute, as many historians believed the slaughter was carried out by bandits disguised as Natives. They contend that the stagecoach's mail sacks were rifled through, something Natives would not have done, as their motives were never robbery, nor did they comprehend the U.S. mail system. Kruger said that the perpetrators stole $25,000 from the plundered stage, but Natives at that time did not understand United States currency. Even at the time, prominent Arizona pioneer Charles Genung expressed his belief the attack was carried out by white men.

The debate continues today, with some historians speculating that miscreants who were not Natives carried out the atrocity. Some have even wondered if the survivors, William Kruger and Mollie Sheppard, were the real murderers, since Kruger's account of their escape sounds so far-fetched. On the other side, the prominent western historian R. Michael Wilson has written two books on the Wickenburg Massacre, in which he claims there is no doubt it was a brutal Native attack.

Kruger would later say that Mollie Sheppard died of her wounds sometime afterward, but there is no record of her death. After the attack, she apparently gave no statements to newspapers, and virtually nothing is known of her life, however long she lived afterward. Some historians believe she had lived a life of prostitution before the massacre, but evidence of this is lacking. Owing to her complete disappearance following the attack, some have speculated that she did not survive for any time at all and may have been one of the victims who was buried. But if this is true, it is not known why William Kruger would falsely claim she had survived.

In 1937, the Arizona Highway Department erected a stone monument near the site of the Wickenburg Massacre, with an inscription blaming "Apache-Mohave Indians," whom the Yavapai tribe was often mistaken for in earlier years. This monument still stands. The actual location of the massacre site has been in dispute as well. The location of the graves of the victims has also been shrouded in mystery, with reports stating their graves have been moved several times. In 2007, the Arizona Pioneer Cemetery Research Project (APCRP), a group that restores neglected and abandoned cemeteries, gathered at what is believed to be the Wickenburg Massacre site. APCRP utilizes grave dowsing, a practice not everyone accepts. But with their dowsing rods, the group identified seven graves of the victims, including one they believe belongs to Mollie Sheppard. They erected markers at the grave sites.

Elizabeth Hudson Smith

One of Wickenburg's pioneer citizens in its early days was a Black woman named Elizabeth Hudson Smith. The daughter of enslaved people, she left the South and learned to read and write. Ending up on Chicago, she married a railroad porter named Bill Smith on September 16, 1896. Bill reportedly worked on the Santa Fe, Prescott and Phoenix Railway (SFP&P).

The Smiths headed west, looking for a new life in an area where they might be more accepted, and they settled in Wickenburg in 1897. At this time, the mining town had a large minority population of Mexicans, Chinese, Natives, et cetera, who worked in the mines, particularly the Vulture.

Finding work at the Baxter Hotel as a cook and bartender, respectively, Elizabeth and Bill eventually purchased the property and renovated it, adding a second story, making it Wickenburg's first two-story building. Elizabeth was an excellent cook, and the townspeople began patronizing the new establishment. It was a success.

The success of the renovated Baxter Hotel attracted the attention of SFP&P officials, who approached the Smiths with a proposal to build a new hotel and restaurant on Railroad Street, closer to the train tracks, where

Wickenburg Hotel Vernetta, circa 1912. *Nancy Burgess.*

passengers could get off and have a meal during stops at Wickenburg. It is unknown who financed the enterprise, but the new hotel was built. It was a two-story brick building with fifty rooms. The Smiths named it the Vernetta Hotel, after Bill's mother.

The new hotel was a big success. According to Arizona historian Jana Bommersbach, Elizabeth always greeted guests personally while dressed in fine clothes, and Bill operated a small saloon in the lobby. Other businesses were available in the town as well, including a bank branch and a post office. However, in 1912, Elizabeth's husband, Bill, walked out on her and never returned. She eventually filed for divorce on the grounds of desertion, and it was automatically granted when Bill did not show up for the hearing.

With the money Elizabeth was making from the Vernetta, she helped construct an opera house in town, Wickenburg's first, and worked to bring touring companies through the area. In the ensuing years, she also purchased a farm to provide meat, fruit and vegetables for the hotel. She invested in mining claims and other businesses in town. The growth of Wickenburg into the modern era was due in large part to the business sense and community leadership of Elizabeth Hudson Smith.

But major changes came with modern times. Wickenburg continued to grow, and more white people came to town from other areas of the country, bringing their prejudices with them. By the 1920s, Wickenburg's white population, including those who had been Elizabeth's friends, began to shun her. Guests began staying at the newer white-owned hotels. To obtain the few guests she could get, Elizabeth had to start dressing as a lowly maid in the Vernetta Hotel.

Elizabeth Hudson Smith died on March 25, 1935, and few noted her passing in the town she had helped build. Her death certificate lists her cause of death as "la grippe" (a type of flu), along with endocarditis. The doctor who filled the certificate contemptuously added, "She should have gone to bed but did not." However, in an October 28, 2020 article in the *Wickenburg Sun* newspaper, Gloria Brewer, who heads the Wickenburg Legends and Ghost Tours group, stated her belief that Elizabeth was poisoned.

Because she was black, Elizabeth was ignominiously buried in the Garcia Cemetery, a burial ground in west Wickenburg that was set aside for mostly racial minorities. According to Jana Bommersbach, Elizabeth was largely forgotten until 1998, when Wickenburg historian and folk singer Dennis Freeman revived her story for his play, *Out Wickenburg Way*. After the show, a very elderly gentleman named Tony O'Brien, perhaps the oldest man alive in Wickenburg at that time, who had known Elizabeth, walked up to the stage with tears in his eyes and cried out to the actress who had played her, "Elizabeth, it's me, Tony!"

Today, the two-story building that was the Vernetta Hotel still stands on Frontier Street (formerly Railroad Street) in Wickenburg. As of this writing, it is now called the Hassayampa Building and stands empty. An elegant mannequin of Elizabeth Hudson Smith has been erected in front of the

Wickenburg Hotel, now the Hassayampa Building, in 2022. *Parker Anderson.*

structure in tribute to her. In Prescott, Arizona, Sharlot Hall Museum has inducted Elizabeth into its Memorial Rose Garden, a tribute bestowed on significant pioneer women who lived in Arizona before statehood was achieved in 1912.

The Wickenburg Chamber of Commerce occupied the Hassayampa Building for a while in the early 2000s, while the old railroad depot (the chamber's current home) was being remodeled. Chamber staff were positive that the sad ghost of Elizabeth Hudson Smith still resides in the building. A figure of a woman looking out the second-story front window has been seen from the outside. Footsteps have been heard on the staircase, and lavender perfume has been smelled when no one was around. The *Wickenburg Sun* article cited previously quoted Julie Brooks, the executive director of the Wickenburg Chamber of Commerce, who said chamber staff believe there are multiple ghosts in the building. While they worked there, lights turned on and off, and they heard doors closing in rooms where the doors were already closed. None of the spirits seem to be malevolent.

Garcia Cemetery

On the west end of town lies the Garcia Cemetery. It was originally established as a burial ground for the victims of the 1890 Walnut Grove Dam collapse (they were interred in an unmarked mass grave). The rest of this graveyard became the place where racial minorities were buried. Wickenburg's cemeteries at that time were racially segregated, with the area's Mexican, Chinese and Black people buried here. This is where Elizabeth Hudson Smith was interred.

The Garcia Cemetery does have a reputation for being haunted, although vivid stories are not common. Generally, visitors sometimes catch glimpses of passing figures out of the corners of their eyes, and when they turn to look, no one is there. This seems to happen most often in the early morning or evening. As with most cemeteries—haunted or not—few people ever try to visit at night.

Chamber of Commerce/Train Depot

Down Frontier Street from the Hassayampa Building/Vernetta Hotel is Wickenburg's old railroad depot, which was built in 1895 and where the trains arrived in bygone days. Now that the depot is restored, the Wickenburg Chamber of Commerce resides here. The old depot is also haunted. In the previously cited *Wickenburg Sun* article, chamber of commerce executive director Julie Brooks was quoted as saying that paranormal teams have investigated the building in recent years and determined there are spirits present. Fortunately, they seem to be friendly.

The Jail Tree

On Tegner Street in downtown Wickenburg, there is a giant and clearly very old tree that has been a tourist attraction since at least the 1940s. Called the Jail Tree, town legends contend that Wickenburg did not have a jail in the nineteenth century and instead arrested criminals and chained them to this tree until authorities from Phoenix could come by to pick them up.

Although documentation for the tree's history is scant, tourists who take pictures here often capture orbs. Paranormal teams have also reported feeling spirit energy here, but unlike most haunted sites in town, the Jail Tree is often said to have negative energy. Perhaps this is due to the criminals who were chained here and now cannot rest. Old jails and prisons are often haunted by negative and angry spirits.

Gloria Brewer (quoted previously) told the *Wickenburg Sun* that on one of her ghost tours, her son started feeling very sick at the Jail Tree. A person on the tour took his photograph, which showed a large red cloud surrounding him. The color red is often an indicator of an angry or negative spirit energy.

The famous "Jail Tree" in Wickenburg now stands as a tourist attraction. *Parker Anderson.*

Antiques and Artists Emporium

Near the U.S. Highway 93 roundabout is a two-story antique store called the Antiques and Artists Emporium. The building used to house the Texas Hotel in its early days. Today, it is an eclectic shop filled with a wide variety of antiques and trinkets. The building was constructed in 1895.

The emporium is haunted, probably by spirits from the building's days as a hotel. The shop owner told the *Wickenburg Sun* that items are moved about regularly during the night, and the sounds of footsteps and other movements can be heard, particularly upstairs. An intuitive customer once told her there are around forty spirits upstairs.

A friend of the owner once told her that one of the spirits was named Allison, and she worked at the Texas Hotel in the 1930s and died of lung disease.

Author Parker Anderson, while on a visit to the emporium with Darlene Wilson in 2021, tried to take a photograph upstairs with his phone. Despite holding the phone still, the photograph turned out blurry and looked like the camera had been aimed at the floor. Perhaps the spirits dislike having pictures taken of their abode.

SOUTHEAST ARIZONA

BISBEE

The mining town of Bisbee has had a long and complex history. In 1877, a man named George Warren filed several copper and silver mining claims in the Mule Mountains and Tombstone Canyon near the Mexican border, some of them on behalf of other miners. This led to the area becoming known as the Warren Mining District. He owned a small share in the Copper Queen Mine, which he reportedly later gambled away.

In 1880, the Copper Queen was acquired by investor Edward Reilly, who sought out other investors to put up the capital to mine the copper ore. He persuaded San Francisco engineers DeWitt Bisbee, William H. Martin and John Ballard to invest heavily in the Copper Queen. As they did around all successful mining areas, a town grew up next to the Copper Queen's activity to serve the miners' needs. The town was named for investor DeWitt Bisbee.

But the success of the Warren Mining District attracted national attention. Mining entrepreneur James S. "Rawhide Jimmy" Douglas was sent by the Phelps Dodge Corporation to investigate the area. Based on his positive reports, Phelps Dodge acquired several of the mines, including the Copper Queen, and formed the Copper Queen Consolidated Mining Company in 1885.

All the mining towns of the era seem to have been beset by violence and lawlessness, and Bisbee was no exception. On the dark night of December 3, 1883, five men, Dan Dowd, Billy Delaney, Dan Kelly, Red Sample and

Water burros were used for hauling water in the Bisbee mines. *Nancy Burgess.*

Tex Howard, forced their way into the Goldwater-Casteneda Store and, at gunpoint, told Joseph Goldwater to open the safe. While three of the bandits were cleaning out the safe, the two standing guard began shooting at passersby who could have been potential witnesses against them. Alerted by the shots, other citizens and a deputy named Tom Smith ran to the scene, where a shootout then erupted. When the smoke cleared, four people, including Deputy Smith and a pregnant woman named Annie Roberts, lay dead, and the bandits had successfully ridden out of town with their loot. A large posse was soon formed to go after them. The incident came to be known as the Bisbee Massacre.

It took a long time, but eventually, in February 1884, the men were caught and brought to Tombstone for trial. During that time, a man named John Heath, who operated a saloon near the Goldwater store, was also arrested as the alleged mastermind of the robbery after he, as a member of the posse, reportedly tried to lead the trackers to a false trail. The five killers were tried and sentenced to hang. Heath was tried separately and was found guilty of second-degree murder and sentenced to life in prison. Outraged by the leniency shown to Heath, a group of angry citizens stormed the jail in Tombstone on February 22, 1884. They dragged Heath down Toughnut Street and hanged him from a telegraph pole. The incident made national news, as mob lynchings were not as common in Arizona as they were in other states at the time. As public sentiment favored the vigilantes, none of them were ever hunted or arrested for the lynching. John Heath has a marker in Boothill Cemetery in Tombstone, but he was not actually buried there. His body was returned to his parents in Terrell, Texas, where he was buried in a cold, unmarked grave in Oakland Memorial Park. Today, some Arizona historians doubt his guilt, believing he was an innocent victim of the anger and hysteria following the Bisbee Massacre.

Meanwhile, on March 25, 1884, the five killers were legally hanged simultaneously in Tombstone and were buried in Boothill Cemetery.

By the turn of the century, the Copper Queen was regarded as perhaps the largest copper mine in Arizona. But a miners' union, Industrial Workers of America, was organized to unionize the workers and fight against abuses and the exploitation of the workers by management. Mining companies across America responded violently to the unions, and Bisbee was no exception. In 1917, Phelps Dodge, with the cooperation of Cochise County sheriff Harry C. Wheeler, used private police to arrest over 1,300 unionized miners and forced them, at gunpoint, across the border to New Mexico and warned them to never return to Arizona. This incident has become known as the Bisbee Deportation.

Bisbee became the Cochise County seat in 1929, but mining output began to decline in the mid-twentieth century, and in 1975, Phelps Dodge shut down the Copper Queen for good. Unlike many mining towns, Bisbee survived the end of mining, and today, it derives most of its economy from tourism. Many of the town's old buildings have been renovated, and the Copper Queen Hotel has become a popular lodging place for visitors.

There are many books and stories that have been written about the ghosts of Bisbee, Arizona. While these stories have been passed down and shared repeatedly, they are still very intriguing. Visiting Bisbee as a paranormal investigator is the most interesting way to experience the town.

Walking the streets of Bisbee at night can be an eerie experience, as you never know when you'll stumble across a ghostly figure or hear strange noises. You can even take a haunted town tour if you're brave enough.

Castle Rock in Bisbee, Arizona. *Nancy Burgess.*

Several stories are intriguing, like those of the ghosts that haunt Clawson House Inn. Built in 1895 by Spencer Clawson, a mine manager, the inn is haunted by his wife. It is a home she loved and has refused to leave. Eventually, the Clawson House Inn was turned into a boardinghouse.

Other spirits roaming the inn are those of three workers who crossed picket lines. The miners were on strike then, so the mining company found unemployed men to do the jobs of the striking workers. The ghosts of the murdered workers are thought to be trapped in the Clawson House, fearful of venturing out and possibly encountering the spirits of the miners. The ghosts of the workers are truly gruesome sights. They are covered in blood from their bludgeoning by shovels and pickaxes. Their eyes glow like red bulbs as they watch for the return of their murderers. It would be best not to provoke them or mention the word *strike*.

Strikers and their supporters used to be deported by the companies that owned the mines, the towns and practically all the town's buildings. They were rounded up, placed on a guarded train and dumped hundreds of kilometers out in the desert. A strike back then was more like a war.

One day, guards came to the Clawson House and warned the strike breakers to come out, since they would only be brought to the train station and sent on their way without being hurt. Instead, the strike breakers allegedly discharged their weapons out the windows. The miners killed the strike breakers after they charged the home.

It is said the paranormal activity of the miners causes discomfort to the guests and employees of the Clawson House Inn. Their presence evokes fear in those who encounter them, whether they appear as vaguely as an eerie, spine-tingling cold spot or as deliberately as a loud crashing sound outside or inside a guest's room.

The Copper Queen Hotel is Bisbee's oldest and most well-known haunted hotel. Built in 1902, it was once a luxurious establishment for miners and their families. The hotel has undergone many changes over the years and has kept many of its original features, including its stained-glass windows and grand staircase.

Today, the hotel is said to be haunted by the ghost of Julia Lowell, a former hotel guest who died of a broken heart. Guests have reported hearing her phantom footsteps in the halls, and her spirit is said to linger in the hotel's bar.

The Shady Dell Vintage Trailer Court was opened in 1927 to provide camping spaces to travelers. Today, it is a vintage trailer park with trailers from the '40s and '50s furnished in period décor. Haunted? Definitely. This hotel is composed of refurbished vintage trailers from the 1950s, and it is said to be haunted by the ghost of a former resident. Guests have reported hearing strange noises and seeing shadowy figures in their rooms. Maybe it is the spirit of a former resident. The trailer court backs up to an old and haunted cemetery. Wonder who will visit you from the cemetery?

The Bisbee Grand Hotel is rich in history and has numerous reports of hauntings. This historic building was built in 1907 and is said to be haunted by the spirit of a little girl, believed to be the daughter of a hotel proprietor. She is said to appear in the lobby, playing with a ball or skipping around. She is often seen wearing a white dress, and her presence is said to be accompanied by a feeling of comfort.

The spirit of the wife of a guest who was staying at the hotel has been seen in the attic and around the stairwells. She is said to wear a long, old-fashioned dress, surrounded by a feeling of sadness.

The ghost of the Bisbee Jail is a popular urban legend that dates to the early 1900s. According to legend, the jail was originally built to hold prisoners. Still, it was soon abandoned due to a series of mysterious and disturbing events. Witnesses claim they have seen a ghostly figure in the jail, said to be the spirit of an inmate who died under mysterious circumstances. Some have even reported hearing strange noises coming from the jail at night, and a feeling of dread has been known to cause people to flee in terror. To this day, the identity of the ghost of the Bisbee Jail remains a mystery.

A historic house located on the corner of Main Street and Tombstone Canyon Road, built in 1895 by a local miner, has been the subject of many local ghost stories. The house is said to be haunted by the ghost of its original owner, a miner named Edward Smith. According to local legend, Smith's ghost still haunts the house and can be heard walking up and down the stairs late at night. Other paranormal activities reported include unexplained noises, cold spots and objects that move independently. The house is now a popular tourist attraction open to the public. Visitors can take a guided tour of the place and learn more about its history and the local ghost stories.

Bisbee, Arizona, is a charming town in the Mule Mountains of southeastern Arizona. It was founded as a copper, gold and silver mining town in 1880 and has since become an eclectic tourist destination. The town is nestled in the valley among the mountains. Its historic downtown area with various examples of Victorian architecture has been preserved. Visitors to Bisbee can explore its many shops, galleries, restaurants and bars and take tours of the many abandoned mines. There are also plenty of outdoor activities, such as hiking, biking, golfing and bird-watching. And for a unique experience, visitors can check out the Queen Mine Tour, where they can explore an authentic underground mine. Bisbee is a great place to explore and experience the culture and history of the Old West.

If you're looking for a haunted place to explore, consider walking the haunted streets of Bisbee. The historic mining town, located in the Mule Mountains of Arizona, is full of old buildings, abandoned mines and ghost stories. So, take that walk through the streets of Bisbee; you never know who or what you might encounter.

CLIFTON/MORENCI

Metcalf and Morenci have significantly impacted the history of Clifton, Arizona. With over three thousand residents, Clifton is a small town in Greenlee County and the county seat. Although Clifton is less well known than other mining towns in the state, it has a unique charm and is home to dozens of historic buildings with their own stories.

The mineral deposits in that area were first noticed by Spaniards who were looking for gold for their country. The gold was not enough for them to stay and mine, and the constant raids by the Apache made it too dangerous for them to stay. The next arrivals were the Mexicans, but the Apache successfully ran them off. Like many other mining towns, Clifton was on Apache territory, and the Apache did not want outsiders on their land.

In 1856, the first mineral discoveries were made by California volunteers pursuing the Apache, and that touched off a twenty-six-year-long war.

In 1872, a band of Apache raided a nearby town in New Mexico, stealing the best horses in the valley. The cavalrymen, led by Captain Chase, were organized into squads and began a pursuit, which led them into a narrow canyon in the pines where two rivers meet. Two soldiers in the squad, Jim and Bob Metcalf, were prospectors. On the trail of the Apache, several of the men noticed the canyon had copper and even found evidence of primitive mining.

Brothers Robert and Jim Metcalf returned to the area, found a rich copper deposit and named the claim Longfellow, since it was founded on the poet's birthday.

Geronimo was part of the Chiricahua Apache community and was born where three rivers meet. Some believed he was born in New Mexico, but his description of where he was born sounds like it is what is now Clifton. The three rivers in the Clifton area are Eagle Creek, the San Francisco River and the Gila River.

It is said Geronimo was born in 1829 and left the Clifton area in 1882, along with two hundred Apache warriors. But the Mexican government started ambushing Apache villages and was getting paid handsome rewards for Apache scalps. Colonel Carrasco and about four hundred Mexican soldiers raided Geronimo's Bedonkohe camp in 1851. They massacred many of its occupants while Geronimo and several other warriors were on a trading mission in the town of Janos. After the massacre, when Geronimo returned home, he discovered the bodies of his mother, wife and three little children and swore revenge. "I had lost all," he stated in his memoirs.

Geronimo and his warriors terrorized the areas within a five-hundred-mile radius for the next four years. Clifton was part of the worst Native conflicts; its ore wagon trains were attacked, the drivers killed and the mules stolen. Geronimo's band also killed eleven Mexican teamsters twelve miles to the south. They attacked the smelter and wagon trains that were trying to reach Clifton with food and supplies.

In 1886, Lieutenant Gatewood convinced Geronimo to give himself up. He was transferred to Florida and then taken to Fort Sill, Oklahoma, where he died in 1909. All he wanted was to return to Arizona, but that never happened.

Clifton was founded in 1873, and the ore coming from Clifton/Metcalf/Morenci was hauled by mule-drawn wagons through Clifton, where it began a long and dangerous journey. When the ore left, Clifton and the wagons were not attacked by the Apache. The wagons, while returning with much-needed supplies, were successful enough to make the round trip back to Clifton, which took months.

Clifton and Metcalf had close connections with the smelter, and Metcalf worked with the mines. Metcalf was named after Robert Metcalf and was founded in 1882. Metcalf sold the mine to the Lezinsky brothers from New Mexico. The brothers began developing the mine and needed a better way to get the ore down the mountain to the smelter in Clifton. They built a railroad, and its incline made transporting the ore faster and easier. But in 1913, a coupling pin on an ore car snapped, sending nine men plummeting to their deaths from 3,300 feet down a 38 percent grade. People watched helplessly on the ledge above the incline as their coworkers sped to their deaths. The ore car was later replaced with a wood-burning locomotive.

Metcalf no longer exists. Today, it is part of the expanding dumping ground of the Morenci Pit. Morenci was once the Joy's Camp, founded in

An overview of the active Morenci Copper Mine in the mountain from Clifton. *Nancy Burgess.*

1872, and with Phelps Dodge acquiring the Arizona Copper Company in 1921, its name was changed to Morenci. The stories of Metcalf and Morenci closely paralleled that of Clifton.

As the area boomed, so did the crime, as it did many mining camps. A stonemason named Margarito Varela was hired to build the Clifton Cliff Jail in 1881. Criminals used to be sent to work in the mines, but with so many escapes, it was time for an escape-proof jail. The Lezinsky brothers commissioned a jail to be built into a granite cliff by Margarito Varela. Varela used a drill, pick and blasting powder to make two cells inside the building: one for more violent prisoners and the other for milder offenders. Massive iron bars were fitted in the cells and the jail's doors. The two cells' windows were ten feet above the floor. The jail didn't look like much, but there was no escaping it.

Constructing the jail was a difficult job, and Varela was so happy to be finished that he decided to celebrate with the money he was paid to build the jail. He went to the local dance hall and got so drunk, he shot up the place, which happened to be owned by a deputy sheriff. This led to his arrest, and he became the first prisoner in his new jail.

The jail was shuttered in 1906. That year's flood nearly submerged the facility. Prisoners had to be dragged out through a tiny window in the roof's highest point. Mud and flood-related debris filled the facility. It was restored in 1929 and is now part of the Clifton Townsite Historic District.

The Clifton Mineral Hot Springs Bath House was built in 1928 and opened for business in January 1929. With the shutdown of the mines and smelter in 1921 and the sale of the Arizona Copper Company to the Phelps Dodge Corporation, the town's economy took a hit. Locals began to search for ways to bring visitors to Clifton. The discovery of the hot springs would bring in the tourists and money they needed.

Clifton Jail was built in 1881 and shuttered in 1906 but was restored in 1929 as part of the Clifton Townsite Historic District. *Pamela Harrington.*

The bathhouse was different from the money-making project they thought it would be, but it brought customers from all over the country to partake in its thermal springs. It also helped other businesses and the social life of Clifton. The town had theaters and opera houses bringing in renowned talent. With the Great Depression, the bathhouse was shut down. It was purchased by Phelps Dodge and used to house various offices.

In 1904, a single train carrying forty Irish orphans, three nuns and four nurses landed in Clifton, Arizona. The local priest was to choose Catholic homes for these orphans. Most Catholic households at the time were Mexican. The white community in Clifton was outraged to see these Irish children turned over to Latino homes. The night the children arrived in Clifton, people began fighting over them. A furious crowd of four hundred gathered to pressure the priest to retrieve the orphans. People were fighting over the children, treating the situation like they were shopping at a bazaar.

Many of these children had been given up by single mothers or families who were too poor to care for them, a legacy of the Irish Potato Famine of

1845. Many Irish families immigrated to the United States, primarily New York. Many willing Catholic families in Clifton wanted children and wanted to help their priests. It was a way for the children to become Americans.

But a crew of twenty-five vigilantes attacked the Mexican homes and abducted the children as a mob gathered. The nuns and twenty-one children fled, the young priest was expelled from the community and the remaining children were sent to new, white, non-Catholic families.

Clifton was no longer part of mining and refining activities. It became a hub for people and shops. In 1890, Clifton had seven saloons, two doctors, several Chinese restaurants, three general stores and opium parlors. Most of the town's population was made up of Mexican, Chinese and Italian people and some Jewish merchants. The town also had several brothels, taverns, hotels and shops that sold various products.

Over the years, Clifton has been struck by devasting disasters, including fires, floods and miners' strikes. Visitors to Clifton will notice the enormous metal gate on the south end of town. Locals call it the Jurassic Park gate. The gate was built in the 1990s to protect south Clifton from flooding.

The flood of 1891 washed away many buildings and caused the railroad tracks to shift; no train could get through for several days. The flood of 1903 was one of the worst to strike the town. While more rain fell in Morenci than

Chase Creek Street in Clifton, Arizona. *Darlene Wilson.*

in Clifton, a wall of water eight feet high came flowing down the canyon. The dam at Morenci that had been built to hold that town's tailings had broken. A man who was delivering groceries to Morenci saw the water rushing down the mountain and raced down to Clifton to warn the town. No one listened to him, and the water struck houses, crumpling them into nothing. The rain lasted for more than an hour, but it took months to build the town back up. A dozen people died, and others were missing but never found.

The most devastating flood occurred in 1906, when it rained for thirty hours. The tailings dam broke again, flooding Chase Creek Street in Clifton and killing eighteen people. The flood was so great that there was talk of abandoning the town. After this flood, the wall along Chase Creek was built using slag and mortar, forming a flood wall sixteen inches deep.

In 1911, the Greenlee Courthouse was built and became the oldest functioning courthouse in Arizona. During this time, Chase Creek structures were destroyed by fire. New buildings were constructed in 1912, and some are still standing today.

In 1983, the area was hit with the worst tropical cyclone in its history, with heavy rains causing many streams to burst their banks. Over seven hundred homes were destroyed, many of the town's businesses were heavily damaged and all the residents of Clifton had to be evacuated.

Many of the area's mining operations were consolidated, starting with the Metcalf and its Longfellow Mine. As mentioned earlier, the mine was sold to the Lezinsky brothers, who sold it to Frank Underwood, who then sold it to the Scottish investors of the Arizona Copper Company. The Detroit Copper Company was established and later became the Shannon Copper Company. Then the Phelps Dodge Corporation became a part owner of the Detroit Copper Company. The mine's current owner is the Freeport McMoRan Mining Company.

Union organizing began in Clifton in 1903, when Mexican laborers joined together to form mutual aid societies. With wartime copper demand so high, more than four thousand workers at several mining companies struck for higher wages and recognition. The mining company agreed to their terms.

In 1942, mine workers formed Morenci Miners Local 616, representing more than three thousand workers, which won its first significant victory following a 107-day strike in 1946. In 1983, a recession sent copper mining into a decline, and Phelps Dodge temporarily laid off its entire Arizona and Texas workforce.

When the strike of June 1983 began at midnight, Phelps Dodge hired replacement workers, causing clashes between strikers, strikebreakers and their families. Two months later, the Arizona governor sent more than 750 law enforcement personnel, 425 state troopers and 325 national guardsmen to keep the peace. In September that year, all strikers were permanently replaced when the most devasting flood happened.

The Clifton Train Station

The Clifton Train Station was started as a narrow-gauge railroad by the Clifton and Lordsburg Railroad in 1883, and over the years, the lines expanded when various railroad companies purchased the railroad.

The Clifton Train Station is a historic landmark that played an essential role in the development of the town of Clifton, Arizona. Built in 1913, the station served as a hub for the Arizona Eastern Railway, transporting copper ore from the nearby mines to other parts of the state and beyond. The station was also a key entry point for travelers coming to Clifton, a booming mining town.

Today, the Clifton Train Station and Visitor Center is a testament to the town's rich history. The station has been beautifully restored to its original grandeur, and visitors can step back in time and experience what life was like in Clifton during its heyday. The station is also home to a museum, which features exhibits on the town's mining history and the role of the railway in the development of the area.

Clifton Train Station was built in 1913 and used for transporting copper ore and passengers traveling to and from Clifton. *Pamela Harrington.*

The Clifton Train Station is an essential part of the town's history and a testament to the ingenuity and innovation of the people who built it. Passenger trains were decommissioned in 1967. The downstairs area of the station was, at various times, a café, a bar, office space and a gathering place for people. The upstairs area has been used as an activity center and a place for dances and has been rented out for offices. The Town of Clifton owns and maintains the building today. It was listed in the National Register of Historic Places in 1990.

The Arizona Copper Company General Office/Elks Lodge Building

The building featured on the cover of this book was constructed in the early 1900s by the Arizona Copper Company (ACC) as its general office. The ACC selected this site at the base of a cliff near its smelting operations for the construction of this two-story headquarters and office building. It faces the main thoroughfare and the San Francisco River.

A 1910 addition to the south end was built, matching the original building perfectly. The Phelps Dodge Company acquired the ACC holdings, and the railway was transferred to its own El Paso and southwestern system. No longer needing offices in Clifton, Phelps Dodge leased the railroad portion of the building to the Gila Valley Bank and Trust Company, which then merged with Valley Bank of Phoenix to become the Valley National Bank. The Clifton branch operated continuously in this location into the 1980s. Phelps Dodge also leased space in the building to the Benevolent and Protective Order of Elks (BPOE), lodge 1174. Around 1970, the Elks built a modern addition to the north side of the building.

In 1983, the strike against Phelps Dodge, coupled with extensive flooding the same year, affected businesses in the former ACC office building. The Valley National Bank shut its branch in 1985, after a landslide damaged the building. Membership of the Elks in Clifton declined, eventually merging with the lodge in Safford.

The building has housed a variety of other organizations, including the Greenlee County Alternative School. Although the original double-hung windows have all been replaced with fixed glazed windows, the structure retains a high degree of integrity. The building was listed in the National Register of Historic Places in 1990 as a contributor to the Clifton Townsite Historic District.

This building was constructed by the Arizona Copper Company in the early 1900s, and then other companies occupied the building, including the Elks Lodge. It is now owned by the Town of Clifton. *Darlene Wilson.*

In 2017, the Town of Clifton added the former ACC/Elks Club building to its properties. Parts of the building are now more than a century old and present opportunities to preserve pieces of Clifton's history. There are no current plans for the building, though the town will allow the Clifton Closet Thrift Store to remain there. As of this writing (2023), renovations are being done to the building for future office space.

Bighorn Sheep in Clifton

Clifton is home to diverse wildlife, including majestic desert bighorn sheep. These magnificent creatures can be found throughout the area and are famous sights among locals and tourists alike. Some locals get frustrated with them because they eat all the plants and flowers in their yards.

Unfortunately, bighorn sheep populations in Arizona and throughout the American West have declined in recent years due to habitat loss and disease. Conservation efforts are underway to protect these magnificent animals. Enhancing the habitat through cooperation with landowners and government agencies is ongoing.

Visitors will see signs around Clifton and Morenci cautioning motorists to drive carefully on the roads. The sheep can appear from nowhere and often get hit and killed by vehicles.

Overall, the bighorn sheep is a beloved symbol of Clifton's natural beauty and a reminder of the importance of protecting the wildlife that make this area special. It is a unique experience to see these majestic animals on the side of the mountains in Clifton. Author Wilson has had that pleasure, and it just takes your breath away. Watching them work their way down the mountains so gracefully is impressive.

The Coronado Trail Route 666

Route 666, known as the Devil's Highway, is now known as Highway 191. Author Wilson was told the Highway 666 signs kept getting stolen, so the transportation departments from New Mexico, Colorado, Utah and Arizona proposed a new name for the state route and changed it to Highway 191.

Clifton is the gateway to the Coronado Trail, a National Scenic Byway with hundreds of miles of hiking trails. The trails soar between six thousand and nine thousand feet in elevation. There are campgrounds scattered around the Apache-Sitgreaves National Forest, and the temperatures can be quite cold in the winter evenings.

Highway 666 is as tortuous, wild and strange as its name, with more than one hundred miles of twisting curves that have caused several travelers to crash off cliffs. It is one of the most scenic roads in the state, with many popular outdoor recreation areas that are not overrun by tourists.

Reports of strange encounters with mad truckers, packs of demon dogs, ghosts and other apparitions have given the route a bad reputation. Some have seen a young woman who haunts the highway. They believe she was killed in a car accident on the highway and now wanders the road in search of her lost love. Some even say they have heard her singing a sad song.

Several people have shared their experiences of a phantom truck that drives down the highway at night with its headlights off. Some call it the ghost truck.

One of the owners of PJ's Café in Clifton shared his story. One of his customers said he was driving the highway from Clifton to Safford when he came upon a hitchhiker carrying a guitar case. He stopped and offered him a ride. The hitchhiker climbed into the truck, and the driver started back down the road, but when he turned to ask the hitchhiker a question, no one was there.

So many residents and shop owners had experienced so many strange activities that they contacted the Travel Channel's *Ghost Hunters*. And on December 2, 2019, a post on Clifton's Facebook page had a call for a "Haunted Town Hall Discussion" with the *Ghost Hunters* Team.

The *Ghost Hunters* group met with the people of Clifton, asking for a show of hands of who had experienced paranormal activity. Everyone in the room raised their hands. One by one, they approached the front and shared their stories.

In author Wilson's opinion, calling the town "Terror Town" is a little harsh. She has visited, stayed and investigated the town many times with her friends and have found much activity, but it has all been informative and exciting.

Wilson and her friends always stay at the Clifton Hotel, which is owned by Karen Crump-Fry and her husband, Matt Fry. They have taken a condemned building, ready to be demolished by the city and completely damaged inside and out and turned it into the most stunning place. When you enter the lobby, you take a step back in time. From velvet wallpaper to clawfoot tubs and stunning lighting, everything was designed after Clifton's early days (except for having a bathroom in every room).

Clifton Hotel was the Central Hotel. It has now been renovated and is a stunning historic hotel. *Darlene Wilson.*

Once known as the Central Hotel and the center of everything, it started as a one-story hotel, but later, another floor was added. The original owner, Julie Pitt, married a judge, and with his busy schedule, she was left to run the hotel. All the rooms were small, just big enough for a bed, a side table and a lamp or candle. They were rooms for sleeping only.

Throughout Wilson's many trips to Clifton, she and her team have stayed in all the rooms. They have recorded voices and answers to their questions that have given specific names and dates—things that were not known before. On her first trip, along with friends and ghost investigators, Lisa Stephenson and Sandy Munz, they got amazing ghost information. The next day, when the team gathered in the open room downstairs, enjoying their coffee and talking to Matt and Karen, they shared what they got. The owners would tell them how correct they were and would even elaborate on the story. They were astonished at the information the investigators got and were very impressed.

During one of their trips, Wilson and her friends had things disappear. Maureen lost her pair of reading glasses. She always keeps them in the outside pocket of her purse. She tore her room apart searching for them. They looked everywhere in the hotel and found nothing. On the day they checked out to return home, Maureen found her reading glasses—in the outside pocket of her purse. On a previous trip, Tom lost his cap, something he wore all the time. About a week later, Karen emailed Wilson saying she had found a cap and asked if it belonged to her group. Yes, it was Tom's hat. He said he would get it on his next trip.

There was a prankster in the hotel, so on the group's next trip, Wilson started to communicate with a spirit who asked to be called Smitty. Smitty shared that he was a miner—"Not one of those miners." He was referring to the copper miners at Morenci Mines. No, he said he was a gold miner, a small man, five foot, two inches tall, with long white hair and a beard. He shared that he loves taking things but that he usually returns them after a while.

Wilson asked him what the most unusual thing he ever took was, and he said, "a girdle," then laughed. He said he liked moving Matt's tape measure around so he had to look everywhere for it. Wilson asked him if he had any items that he hadn't returned, and he said, "Karen's knives." He had two of her knives. When I asked Karen if she was missing any utensils, she said, "Yes, two steak knives." She pulled out her utensil drawer and she had only two knives when it was a set of four. She ordered more knives, because Smitty never returned them.

Smitty said his favorite thing to do was hang out in the bar. When two people were at the bar drinking, he would squeeze between them, and when they weren't looking, he would move their drink glass just a little bit so that when they reached for it, it had moved ever so slightly. He loved doing that.

Another spirit the team met there was in the women's bathroom. Sandy and Wilson went in there to ask questions, and the spirit of a young woman said her abusive boyfriend had killed her and thrown her into the river. She had run away from him and ended up in Clifton. She stayed at the hotel in a room that is now the women's bathroom. She said she loved the hotel; it was so fun and busy all the time and always had music. She loved the music. She was talking about the previous hotel, the Central Hotel. It was the center of everything; it held weddings and town meetings, happy people and travelers were in and out all the time. The woman would have been at the hotel in the early 1920s due to how she was dressed. She had short black hair and wore a red flapper dress and an old-fashioned perfume. (Guests have said they smell perfume in the women's restroom.) She was a beautiful young woman, so desperate to get away from the abuse. She thought she had succeeded until one night, when he found her. She said she'll never leave this happy place and its music.

The group also conducted investigations at the Elks lodge across the river from the hotel. The following is a small part of one of their recordings.

Q. Who is here with us?
A. Girl. Sleep. They're coming.
Q. Who's coming?
A. Be quiet. They're our daughters. [Footsteps.]
Q. What is your daughter's name?
A. Terry.
Q. Did you say Terry or Mary? Are you Mary?
A. Who? That's not it. Out. Hurry. Get up. Are you coming? Follow me. She's too scared.
Q. Who's scared?
A. Stand up. Help them.
Q. Help who?
A. What? It's almost time.
Q. Almost time?
A. You see.
Q. See what?
A. I died.

Q. You died?
A. I'm overdone. Here. Leave it and rest.
Q. Are you leaving us?
A. You're leaving?
Q. Are you leaving?
A. Out the back door. Yes. See ya. That's cool about it
[Session ended.]

Then the group met up with Erin Spears and Pamela Harrington. They are locals who are passionate about the history of their beautiful corner of Arizona and the founders of Haunted Arizona Ghost Tours of Clifton, Arizona. Erin has been a Clifton resident for nearly a decade, and Pamela has resided in the stunning lower valley of Greenlee County for nearly twenty years. Together, they love bringing the people and places of bygone eras to life in fun and interactive haunted history tours and events, including dinner mystery theater productions, articles, books, classes and more, through local community organizations.

The following are stories about Clifton that were shared by Pamela Harrington.

Stories of Clifton and Morenci

Pamela Harrington

https://hauntedarizonaghosttours.com/

From ponderosa pines to high desert mountainscapes, Greenlee County's landscape is as varied as its history. Greenlee County has been home to the Mogollon culture, Apache warriors, farmers, cowboys and miners. The following are some stories that my friend and colleague Erin Spears and I have collected over the years.

The Tale of the White Lady

Today, north of Morenci on Highway 191 one can find an overlook that opens up to the large expanse of the current mining operations of the Freeport McMoran Company. There, dump trucks larger than two-story houses appear as minuscule ants in the man-made crater that is colored in various hues of red, brown and gold.

Little do people know that the place that is now lovingly called "the pit" by its workers was once a thriving town that, at one time, rivaled Bisbee and Jerome in fame. Old Morenci, as well as its sister town Metcalf, once boasted beautiful Victorian-style homes, an elite social club, schools, churches and a company store. However, by 1983, the towns had been dismantled and demolished to make room for the expansion of open-pit mining.

However, the former residents still roam their beloved streets dressed in their turn-of-the-century garb. Many workers have witnessed men, women, and children wandering about the open pit, going about their activities as they had done in life; however, one of these residents has earned the notoriety of being the woman in white.

Just north of the open pit, where large trucks cross under the highway bridge, people have seen a woman dressed in white. They have witnessed her jumping off the bridge, but when they go to find her body, she has disappeared.

However, she doesn't merely stay near the bridge. One truck driver related the experience he and a friend had while they got off of their breaks and returned to their respective trucks. As the driver looked across at his friend's truck, he noticed that he was having trouble starting it. He then saw the woman in white standing against the truck. A moment later, she disappeared, and the truck was able to start as if there was nothing wrong with it.

La Llorona

La Llorona, the wailing woman, is said to haunt the waterways of the Southwest from Old Mexico to Colorado. Ghost or demon, this entity has made her presence known along the banks of the San Francisco River, which runs through the heart of Clifton.

Deceptively calm, the San Francisco River has claimed many victims with its unpredictable currents and gnarls of vegetation hidden in its tumultuous, murky water. However, residents of Clifton have come face to face with a woman they describe as sitting alone by the river, crying. When they approach, they find a being straight from a nightmare waiting for them.

One such resident was a child who didn't know the tales of La Llorona, and upon seeing this woman crying, he went up to her to see what was wrong. To his horror, the woman crying was described as having no face, and she tried to grab hold of him. Fortunately, he was able to escape.

Others have had similar experiences, and in one case, the intended victim was pursued until they made it to the safety of the hills, far away from her domain, which lies in the narrow river valley north of the Zorilla Bridge.

The Cardboard People

Before the turn of the century, when the Arizona Copper Company and the Detroit Copper Company ruled this secluded section of Arizona, people throughout the world were recruited to come work in the underground mines of the copper hills. From Italy to Scotland and Mexico to Spain, people arrived on the rails for the promise of a good wage and better life for them and their families.

With the arrival of so many immigrants from so many places, Clifton, Morenci and the surrounding areas soon became a stratified cauldron, with each race living alongside but not among each other.

The Union Pacific Railway also attracted people from the Asian continent. After the railway's completion, many were hired by the major mining companies of Clifton and Morenci to work in the underground mines at a lower wage than the wage white and Latino people received.

The pay scale used by the mines was a tiered system based on race, with Asian individuals earning the least. With this influx of people from China, white and Latino workers soon found that their livelihoods were going to be threatened, since the company cared more about its bottom line than the safety or care of its workers.

Atrocities against Asians skyrocketed, and the newspapers from that time contain many stories about dead "China men" being found after purposeful tunnel collapses and shootings in the streets. Names were very seldom attributed to the victims of the crimes, and many perpetrators got away with murder.

Miners and cowboys would refer to the Chinese as "cardboard people," those who are seen but never fully recognized as fellow human beings. They were easily employed—easily disposed of.

Eventually, the mines caved to the demands of the white and Latino workers and discontinued hiring Asians. Many left to find better opportunities elsewhere, but the ones who stayed filled niches, growing coveted vegetables in their meticulously maintained gardens, becoming dishwashers and operating illegal gambling rings and opium dens.

Today, in the secret underground tunnels and forgotten alleyways of Clifton, people can still hear the muffled words of the Chinese, who were forced into the shadows of Clifton's early history.

The Tale of Two Hotels

Near the heart of Clifton, just over the Zorilla Bridge, sits the historic Clifton Hotel, which dates to before the turn of the century. The building has seen the best and worst of Clifton's past, and in the days when Park Avenue was Conglomerate Avenue, it was known as the Central Hotel, the finest hotel in the region. Julia and George Homeyer, Clifton arrivals in the 1880s, commissioned its construction in 1890, using slag bricks from the copper smelter down the road. Julia became the sole proprietor of the establishment, taking care of all aspects of its operation even after the death of her husband in 1901. There, she remained until 1940, caring for her guests and beloved hotel.

If you have a chance to stay a night at this beautifully restored hotel, Julia will make sure that you still have an exceptional stay, as she is still seen overseeing her hotel and keeping other former guests in line.

Down the road from the current Clifton Hotel sits the eroding foundation of the original Clifton Hotel, owned and run by the Abrahams family. Legend and notoriety are associated with Laura and Sam Abrahams, the proprietors of the hotel and main instigators of a tragedy that still haunts Clifton. Although they were well respected and esteemed in the community in the early 1900s, the Abrahamses were partially responsible for the infamous Arizona Orphan Abduction. In an atmosphere where racial tensions were at a breaking point, the abduction of Catholic foundling hospital orphans from Latino families who lawfully adopted them by Protestant socialites made international headlines.

WILSON CONCLUDES THAT CLIFTON is alive and well and continues to grow. Visit it for yourself and stay in the beautifully renovated and haunted Clifton

Hotel or other lodging or RV Park. Enjoy the best food at PJ's Café and hike the many trails surrounding the area. You'll fall in love with this historical town and its people.

COCHISE

Cochise is a ghost town that was not a mining camp. It was created in the 1880s as a water and fuel stop for the Southern Pacific Railroad. However, it became a shipping depot for the surrounding mining camps. A road was constructed to accommodate the ore shipments that were freighted to and from Cochise for many years.

Cochise's section station was converted into a shipping depot, and a road was built to handle the ore shipments. For many years, the copper ore was shipped by freight to Cochise. A lumber mill was erected close to the train tracks in 1899.

A sign on the highway for the Cochise Hotel. *Darlene Wilson.*

Cochise Hotel was built in 1896. *Darlene Wilson.*

With ore moving out and people and goods pouring in, the town of Cochise expanded quickly as a shipping hub. In 1897, Cochise had a store, post office, dining establishment and meat market. Joe Davis started the first saloon that same year.

The owner of the Cochise Hotel, Phillip Gessert, purchased the Cochise Hotel from the Amerind Foundation in 2013. His family and friends have been his most incredible supporters and business partners. Phillip Gessert is a western historian and author. He worked in Hollywood for over forty years. He kindly permitted the authors of this book to use the stories he has shared on his website. The Cochise Hotel is a bed-and-breakfast and museum. For more information, visit http://cochisehotel.net/index.html.

John J. Rath arrived in 1894 and became the telegrapher for the railroad. He was later known as the father of Cochise. When he arrived in town, he purchased 312 acres of land. He and his wife decided to sell their real estate and create the town. In August 1896, John J. Rath started building the Hotel Rath. It opened for business in November that year. He later renamed it Cochise Royal Hotel and Water Works. Today, it is known as the Cochise Hotel, and you can book a room there or even partake in the haunted events at the hotel. Later, the Henderson Saloon and Cochise Dining Hall opened, offering the town gambling and a bar and restaurant.

Nearby, the towns of Pearce and Gleeson became popular mining camps, attracting miners and families to the area. Cochise became the shipping hub for the ore of the surrounding mining towns. John Rath served as the town's railroad agent, Wells Fargo agent, justice of the peace and postmaster.

In 1901, Rath petitioned for the formation of a school district, and the first school election took place that March. Of course, John Rath was elected to the school board, along with Halerman and Bentley.

John died in a freak accident in 1905 while he was riding in a rented buckboard. John was sitting with his loaded shotgun next to him; the wagon hit a rough spot, and his shotgun discharged, shooting him on the right side of his neck and killing him instantly. His death was ruled to be accidental.

Rath's widow, Lula, and her three daughters returned to Cochise briefly before going to live with her brother William Olney. In 1907, Lula returned to Cochise, assumed the postmaster's responsibilities and reopened the hotel. She also began to sell her lots, seventy-five total, for twenty dollars per lot. She also married Charles Corness, the minister of the Gospel Church in Tombstone.

In early 1913, Lula and Charles Corness sold the Cochise Hotel to Yancy Womack and moved to Los Angeles, California. Lula died in 1966 at the age of ninety-one. The Womack family sold the Cochise Hotel in 1919 to the Skinner family. They owned and operated the hotel for nearly forty years. They made many improvements to the hotel, including the addition of porches on the front and back, a kitchen and a great room. The hotel also had a water closet with a lavatory, tub and hot water.

By the end of World War II, the town of Cochise was on a downswing, and the Cochise Hotel was beginning to show its age. The new interstate bypassed the town, cutting off a significant part of its travel business. The mines had tapped out, and the cattle shipping business went to another town, Willcox, Arizona.

When Ma Skinner passed, the Cochise Hotel remained in the family and was taken over by her daughter, Fern Moore.

The Cochise Hotel changed hands again to Elizabeth Gunter in 1958. Restoration work was started immediately. Modern baths and heaters were installed in each room, and the kitchen was modernized. Elizabeth Gunter soon became Mrs. Husband. Her family was the Fulton family of steam engine fame, and she was one of the wealthiest women in America at that time.

After Elizabeth's husband passed, her trust took over the hotel, and her grandchildren worked to keep the inn alive. In 2007, complications ended their tenure as hosts of the hotel. They removed all the family's belongings and closed the hotel. The Amerind Foundation assumed ownership and put it on the market. It sat empty and abandoned for nearly seven years. The hotel's current owner, Phillip Gessert, began renovations that are never-ending.

The town of Cochise had changed by the 1920s. The 1920 census did not include the inhabitants from 1900. A new group had come, but they had already left.

Today, the population of Cochise is around 1,600. It's another once-booming town with many thriving businesses and families that is now smaller, quieter and more peaceful. It is still home to many residents, businesses and historic buildings, including the Cochise Hotel, the Cochise Church and Cemetery, the former Cochise Train Depot, the post office and the schoolhouse.

The Cochise Hotel is full of stories, and one of author Wilson's favorites is that of "Big Nose Kate."

In 1899, the Raths hired a housekeeper, Mary Katherine Cummings, to run the Cochise Hotel. It is unknown if Lula Rath knew who Mary Cummings was or that she was known as Big Nose Kate, the on-again, off-again girlfriend of Doc Holliday.

Lula's father, Joseph Olney, was a member of the Cowboy Gang and was a bitter enemy of Doc Holliday and the Earp brothers. The 1882 census lists John Ringold (also known as Johnny Ringo), Ike and Phin Clanton and seven-year-old Lula Belle living in Joseph Olney's home. Ringo and the Clantons are believed to be the men who ambushed and killed Morgan Earp and wounded Virgil Earp after the famous shootout at the OK Corral in Tombstone in 1881.

There was a younger Earp brother, Warren Earp. He worked as a cattle detective, rooting out rustlers and cattle thieves. On July 6, 1900, Warren Earp argued with his close friend Johnny Boyett. Warren had learned Boyett was being paid $150 to kill him. After much back and forth, Boyett shot Warren through the heart, killing him instantly.

It is rumored that by August 1900, Wyatt Earp had traveled from Alaska and met up with his brother Virgil Earp at the Cochise Hotel to investigate the murder of their brother Warren. Wyatt was still a wanted man from various warrants that were issued twenty years earlier. Wyatt was careful to remain anonymous while in Arizona. Working at the Cochise Hotel, Big Nose Kate gave the Earps a place to stay and where they could come and go as they pleased in Willcox, where their brother had been killed.

After their investigations, they discovered their brother was a bully of a man and deserved what he got. Virgil and Wyatt left without a trace.

After Big Nose Kate was fired by Lula Rath for reasons unknown, she became a housekeeper for John J. Howard in 1910 and moved to Dos Cabezas, just across from Cochise. When Howard died in 1930, Kate was the executrix of his estate. In 1931, at the age of eighty, she contacted her friend, Governor George Hunt of Arizona, and applied for admission to the Arizona Pioneer Home in Prescott. She was admitted as a resident of the home. She died on November 2, 1940, and was buried at the Arizona Pioneer Home Cemetery in Prescott, Arizona, under the name Mary K. Cummings.

Author Wilson knows the Cochise Hotel is haunted. Guests who have stayed in the hotel have reported hearing cries for help and sobs. They have seen the apparition of a woman's head encased in a glowing ball of light floating throughout the hallways at night. The spirit of a lady of the night has been seen in the front bedroom of the hotel.

Paranormal groups visit and investigate the hotel. Surprisingly, they share similar stories about the spirits they see. A woman has been seen sitting in a rocking chair, rocking back and forth. Another spirit of a woman lives in one of the outbuildings and says she will not leave.

The hotel hosts events yearly, from tours to casino nights and haunted events. The hotel is open by appointment only. Contact the hotel's website, http://cochisehotel.net/index.html, for more information. It's worth the visit.

The historic train depot at Cochise has its own ghost story. Train robbery was very popular in Arizona, although a law was passed making the crime punishable by death. In 1898, Express Messenger Charles Adair killed an overly adventurous train robber. The robber's ghost still wanders the tracks, pacing back and forth, waiting for the train's arrival. He always appears near the tracks where he was shot.

COURTLAND

The ruins of Courtland can be found fourteen miles northeast of Tombstone. Courtland was regarded as one of Arizona's most promising copper camps, because the surface conditions of the region suggested the presence of a copper mother lode.

The town was named after Courtland Young, one of the Great Western Mining co-owners, and founded in 1909. It was situated on the southeast corner of the Dragoon Mountains by W.J. Young, Courtland Young's brother.

The new town of Courtland was made available to investors on a morning in late February 1909. It was mainly businesspeople who wanted to purchase a lot there. To get the best pick, a line of more than one hundred people began forming the previous evening. First come, first serve applied to sales. By June 1909, Courtland had developed into a friendly community. At its height, Courtland had two thousand residents and all the amenities one would expect from a town anywhere.

More miners and their families migrated to the region as significant veins of copper ore were discovered. There were variously positioned houses, most of which were portable tents or what were then referred to as house tents.

In June 1909, the Courtland Jail was constructed due to an event involving a Mexican man who was held captive in the previous jail, or a little abandoned mine shaft with a wooden door. On the morning of June 2, 1909, the inmate tried to flee by setting fire to his mattress, which he had propped up against the entrance. Deputy John Henry Bright brought the prisoner breakfast the following morning, but he had to drag him out because he was comatose.

Steel and reinforced concrete were used to construct the new jail. Its composition included at least some leftover materials, like rails and railroad ties. The structure held two cells, each containing a toilet and a sink. It cost the city of Courtland $1,000 to build the new jail.

Some miners found spending the night in jail appealing, because most people in Courtland slept in shacks or tents. Even though only four to eight prisoners were detained at once, this led to overpopulation. The town court established a system that gave offenders time off their sentence in exchange for repairing roadways. Since many prisoners preferred to remain behind bars rather than find employment, this led to further issues. Records show that the county had to spend a sizable sum of money to feed the prisoners, who referred to the jail as the Bright Hotel.

A post office was established in the town on March 13 that year, and the *Courtland Arizonian* published its first issue. When Courtland became a ghost town, it had important buildings, like homes, motels, the county branch jail, a car dealership, an ice cream parlor, a movie theater, a baseball field and a horse racing track.

The town's boom was short-lived. Within ten years, the mines' profitability started to decline, and in 1921, there was a mass exodus from Courtland. The Dragoons at first appeared to be rich in copper. One mine shaft after another was dug into a three-hundred-foot stratum of limestone starting in 1917. The mines were ultimately abandoned because of this, while a post office remained operational until September 30, 1942.

The Arizona Land Project bought Courtland's historic town and patent mining claims in 2017 to preserve the ghost town's history. The nonprofit, operating under the moniker Courtland Ghost Town, carries out continuous class III cultural resource studies that are required to qualify Courtland for the National Historic Register. The town of Courtland and its stories are critical to Arizona's history, so tours of the abandoned town are now provided, allowing tourists to visit pre-Hispanic Hohokam bedrock mortars, a twentieth-century copper acid leach plant and a nineteenth-century mine. Named one of Arizona's top thirteen ghost towns in 2018, Courtland Ghost Town was highlighted in *Arizona Highways* magazine.

It is worthwhile to study Courtland's brief yet fascinating history. It illustrated the rivalries between massive railroads and mining operations and those between startups and established companies. Even though there was only one murder there, there were a lot of shootings on the town's streets and in neighboring arroyos. The town's modest ruins capture a way of life and a century's worth of history. From the Old to the New West, it can be characterized by its trails, roads and borders, as well as its nineteenth-century railroads and twentieth-century freeways, small homestead farms and larger corporate farms.

Today, the Courtland Jail is the only building still on the town site. Many structures were sold, moved and used elsewhere or demolished. A partial cement sidewalk can still be seen. The sidewalk was built in front of the stores, where residents would stroll and window shop. A few other ruins of what were the offices of the Great Western Copper Company stand just outside of what was the town.

Courtland Jail ruins. The jail was built in 1906. *Darlene Wilson.*

Courtland building ruins. It was once a thriving mining town, but today, not much is left. It is just a glimpse of what it once was. *Darlene Wilson.*

When Wilson and her friends explored the old Courtland Jail, they found graffiti painted on the walls. It is the only building left standing in town. Were they able to sense any spirits in the jail? Not really. They were more in awe of what the town once represented and what it is today.

There were old-timers who liked to share stories they had heard over the years. Are they true? They believed they were. One of their favorites was that of a man who died in a bar brawl. He was a regular and was well liked by the folks in the saloon. One evening, the man and another customer had a confrontation that quickly became fatal. The man was killed in the fight, but his body disappeared. Since then, the townspeople believe his spirit roams the area where the bar once was.

Many of these abandoned mining towns have stories of a miner's ghost that roams the streets. Do the spirits still see the town as it was? Are they looking for their friends or family?

As Wilson and her group left the Courtland area, they were humbled by what it once was and felt a bit of sadness for what it is now—remembering what this town achieved, what it stood for and how it mattered to where Arizona is today.

GLEESON

The Apache ruled this area for years. Although they were not miners, they negotiated deals with other Native tribes, giving them the right to extract turquoise in certain regions. They were believed to be mining in that area in the 1850s and for several decades afterward.

In the 1880s, Tiffany and Company became interested in the turquoise mines when it created a fashion craze for the polished blue-green stone. It became quite the fashion, and the turquoise mines were reopened. The original name for the town was Turquoise, Arizona. It even had its own post office from 1890 to 1894. But as with most fashion crazes, the prominence of turquoise didn't last long, and soon, the mines were forgotten.

Now, the popular mineral was copper, which was abundant in that area. Although silver and gold were found, the copper brought in the miners and prospectors.

John Gleeson purchased a mine in this area and opened a new post office, naming the town after himself. The population was about five hundred at that time. He expanded the mine to a much larger scale. He owned the mine

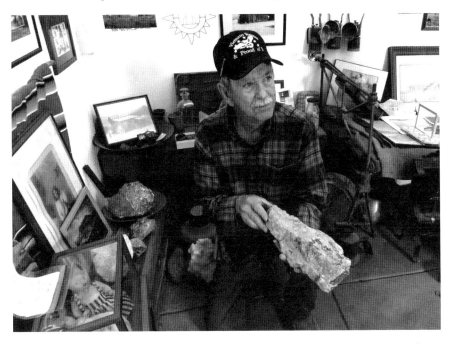

Joe Bono of Gleeson holding a huge piece of turquoise that was mined in the surrounding mountains. *Linda Dershem.*

105

until 1901, when he leased it to a copper company that owned multiple claims on surrounding land.

In 1912, a devastating fire burned down an entire town block on both sides of the road, consuming twenty-eight buildings. But like so many towns in Arizona that were ravished by fire—and there were many—Gleeson rebuilt with brick and concrete instead of wood.

Mining was an important factor in developing that area, causing the economy and population to explode. With ore's decline in the 1950s, the mining companies abandoned the district. With them went the rail service and its railroad tracks.

At one time, Gleeson had all the amenities of a big city. There were hotels, a mercantile store, a movie theater, a roller skating rink, an impressive hotel, a red-light district, several saloons and even a Chinese restaurant owned by Yee Wee.

Gleeson's only jail was a huge oak tree in a wash with a cable. Constable Wes Cates enforced the law then, and he chained prisoners to the cable, where they would stay, day and night, rain, shine or snow.

The town eventually built a jail made of wood and a tin roof in 1906. But in 1910, three prisoners tore off part of the roof and escaped—but not for long. So, in 1910, the town replaced the wooden jail with the existing building.

In 1917, when the United States became involved in World War I, copper was in great demand, and by 1918, Gleeson's population reached six thousand. But with the end of the war and the demand for copper now gone, miners were laid off, and the mines were closed. Many left town to seek jobs in other areas.

In 1938, parts of the movie adaptation of the Zane Grey novel *The Mysterious Rider* were filmed in Gleeson. But by 1939, the town was dying. The post office was closed, the last mine was closed in 1957 and Gleeson had become a ghost town.

Most of the buildings are gone except for the jail, thanks to Tina Miller and John Wiest. Every day, they would drive past the jail on their way to work from their home in Gleeson. They were the owners of the Tombstone Mercantile Company in Tombstone.

In 2008, Tina and John purchased the Gleeson Jail and ten acres of land. They began the restoration of the historic property. Getting it structurally sound was the priority. Repairs of the roof and structural beams were next. The windows had to be rebuilt and a door had to be replaced. Bit by bit, the interior was filled with artifacts from the early 1900s. Stories were collected

The Jail Tree had a cable secured around its trunk, and prisoners were chained by the wrist to the cable. *Darlene Wilson.*

Gleeson Jail was built in 1910, restored in 2008 and is now owned by Joe Bono. *Linda Dershem.*

from local historians, and Tina's background and attention to detail have helped re-create the Gleeson jail.

In 2014, they sold the jail to Joe Bono. Joe Bono was born in Gleeson, and his father owned the Bono General Store just across the road from the jail. Only a small section of the store is standing today. Author Wilson and her friends visited Gleeson in November 2022 and met up with Joe Bono at the Gleeson Jail. It originally had two cells, each with a barred interior door and barred windows on the side and back. At any given time, two to eight inmates would be confined there; they were mostly arrested for petty theft, public drunkenness or assault. Some were being transported to Tombstone. One cell at one time was used as a secure lockup for confiscated bootleg liquor during Arizona's Prohibition period (1915–21). In 1938, the film *Mysterious Rider* filmed a lynch mob scene here.

Joe Bono owns forty acres of land in Gleeson, including the ruins of the old schoolhouse where he and his family attended school. He took the group on a four-wheel ride all around Gleeson. He took them up to an old mine shaft, and they walked around very carefully due to the open holes.

The Joe Bono building was constructed to house an outlet store run by Charles M. Renaud, who owned stores in Courtland and Pearce. It also served as a gas station, a hotel and a general curio shop. For most of its life, it was a saloon. With all the history of this building, it is sad to see it at the point of collapse.

Joe took Wilson and her friends to the ruins of the Gleeson School, built in 1918. It was a massive two-story building. At one time, there were four teachers and scores of students. The last classes were held in 1945.

The Jail Tree mentioned previously still has the cable where the prisoners were chained. The tree has grown over parts of the cable, but it still runs across the wash. Joe told the group that his father said passing children used to throw rocks at the prisoners.

The Shannon Mining Company, which owned the big mines in the area, erected a hospital and made it accessible to its workers in 1913. Only there could miners, ranchers and their families receive medical care for their ailments. Several patients were treated at the hospital during the Spanish flu pandemic (1918–20), and many of them recovered. The hospital had electricity as well. It also had a pit, where, after an amputation, body parts were buried, but the local wildlife would later enter the pit and dig the parts up. The hospital started burning the body parts in the pit to keep the animals away.

Wilson and her friends drove by an old, abandoned trailer home where a man called Bigfoot once lived. He was a giant of a man who, along with his accomplice, brutally murdered two thirteen-year-old girls, Mary and Mandy. On July 4, 1991, at a community celebration where families gathered, camped out and enjoyed festivities, the girls disappeared. The details of their brutal deaths are gruesome and inappropriate for this book. One of the men was sentenced to death, and the other, the codefendant, was sentenced to twenty years in prison. Richard Dale Stokley, age sixty, was pronounced

The Bono Store was originally built as a Gleeson outlet. The building is crumbling now. *Darlene Wilson.*

These were once a busy mine and its tailings. Joe Bono offers tours to these locations; otherwise, they should not be visited, as they are located on private property. *Darlene Wilson.*

dead in the state prison in Florence, Arizona, and Randy Brazeal served his sentence. Afterward, he was released and never seen again.

It was a great afternoon for Wilson and the group, hearing Joe Bono's stories. He showed them pictures of his family and people who lived in the area and enjoyed remembering his time growing up there.

The Gleeson Cemetery is located just down the street from the jail. It is still taken care of, with its most recent burial occurring in 2008. Many locals, including Eugene Yoakem, the final resident of the neighboring ghost

town of Courtland, were buried there. According to one legend that was told to Joe by a local, Joe Bono's grandfather staggered out of the Bono Saloon after getting too drunk and opted to sleep it off and put his horse in a small corral. The following morning, he discovered that he had confined the animal inside one of the cemetery's gated sections.

Today, only a few people live in the area. You can still see the old tailings piles, shafts and water towers that were left behind. Contact Joe Bono at the Gleeson Jail to set up a tour or participate in its events.

There have been numerous reports of hauntings in Gleeson from tourists or paranormal research groups. One person said she thought the ghost of a prior prisoner who died while serving his time haunted the jail.

Some visitors have mentioned feeling cold areas, hearing unusual noises and even seeing apparitions.

For author Wilson, walking through the jail was somewhat unnerving. Certain places are colder than others, and one can feel the difference in the energy. There are so many artifacts and images from earlier times that have stories to tell—if someone would just listen.

When Joe took the group to the old schoolhouse ruins, it reminded Wilson of a story she heard about the ghostly figure of a former student who died in a tragic accident. While searching through old records, she couldn't find any story about an accident, but she has also found that not all stories were printed in the newspapers back then.

Whether or not you believe in the paranormal, the intriguing location appeals to both history fans and ghost hunters due to its rich past and eerie legends. Make plans with Joe Bono if you're interested in investigating or learning more about the history of the region. Keep in mind that everything is private property, and please respect that.

GLOBE

Globe, one of the older mining towns in Arizona, was established in late 1876. Seven hundred people called it home at the time. The town began due to the region's mining, and its open-pit copper mines are still operational today. Globe is the county seat of Gila County, with a population of 7,249, and it is known as the Miami-Globe Mining District.

Like many other mining stories in this book, this one takes place in what was Apache territory. The Apache were too numerous and kept the Spaniards and Mexicans from establishing mines in this region. In the 1820s, the mountain men recognized the area's mineral wealth, but they feared the Apache and left the area.

Several prospecting expeditions attempted to reach the prospective gold mines in the Pinal Mountains in the late 1860s. Some even had the cavalry from Fort Apache escort them. They discovered valuable minerals, but the Apache did not like all of this activity and encouraged them to leave. The prospectors turned around and went back to safety.

In 1871, the army conducted numerous expeditions into the region to subdue the Apache. When the white men from Tucson savagely invaded the peaceful, sleeping Apache camp, it was a terrible incident and became

Mining today in the Globe Miami area. *Darlene Wilson.*

known as the Camp Grant Massacre. There were 144 casualties, almost all of whom were women and children. Many were outraged, and even Ulysses S. Grant, then the president of the United States, condemned the action. Later that year, a trial was held, and all the offenders were cleared. Lieutenant Whitman, who was responsible for all the burials and attempted to console the Apache, was utterly distraught. He was forced out of the army and court-martialed as a result of his compassion.

Another attempt was made by the San Carlos Apache to forbid excursions onto their land. They were initially effective, but the campaign of the new general, General George Crook, almost brought a halt to the overall Apache resistance. The miners were determined, and nothing could hold them back.

Another prospecting expedition into the Pinal Mountains was made in 1873, and miners started to file claims. A few of these early successful men rose to prominence in Globe. Tucson residents created a petition to altogether remove the mining sector from the San Carlos Apache American Reservation. The territory was isolated from the reservation as a result of the agreement. The Globe Mining District was created out of it.

Several smaller mines in Globe started extracting copper ore in the late 1870s, and the Old Dominion Copper Company was established around 1880. Then in 1881, Globe began its most successful venture: copper mining. The Old Dominion Mining Company built a new furnace, and business was good.

The mine and the town of Globe did not fare well in the 1890s. Several homes and businesses were devastated by a flood that swept through the town in 1891; several years later, another flood caused more severe destruction. The town and mine had additional difficulties due to the 1893 financial panic, and mining was halted at the Old Dominion until copper prices went up.

Aerial trams transported ore from smaller mines to a smelter outside of town. As they were in many mining towns, these were challenging times for the Globe area. The Old Dominion Mining Company had some of the best and newest copper mining facilities in place by the early 1900s. The Old Dominion recorded new production totals and revenues by establishing six new smelters. Up to two million pounds of copper per month were hauled out by trains.

Despite the pleasant times, issues still cropped up. Further flooding, a fire and underground mishaps occurred in the mine and town. A strike in 1917 caused such division among the town's miners, proprietors and residents that four companies of federal troops were dispatched and camped in Globe.

Eventually, a settlement was reached, and by 1919, the Old Dominion Corporation employed close to 1,500 people. On the other hand, mine upkeep was disregarded, and water damage and falling copper prices led to a steady decline that reduced employment. Financial problems worsened, and the mine was permanently closed when the Old Dominion Mining and Smelting Corporation could not repay its loan to Phelps Dodge.

During its operation, the mine generated gross revenues of $134 million and produced approximately 800 million pounds of copper. The mine's structures and machinery were auctioned or applied in other facilities.

Although many old structures are in poor condition, many still exist. The Gila County seat's administrative offices are still located in the lovely 1906 courthouse.

The Old Dominion Mining Company's land has been beautifully transformed by the community into a hiking and recreation area, but it has retained part of its mining history.

It's interesting to learn that Globe was home to a well-known South American citizen in 1909. The man identified himself as William T. Phillips when he arrived in Globe, and he had recently wed Gertrude Livesay in Iowa. Several historians, though not all, concur that Phillips's real identity was Robert Leroy Parker, better known as Butch Cassidy. To make sure that his new alias would last, he had traveled to Globe. Many people think Cassidy escaped a shootout in San Vicente, Bolivia, around 1908 and returned to the United States to start a new life. He worked on ranches and in construction while residing in Globe. He departed Arizona for Washington State in the late summer of 1910, and on July 20, 1937, he passed away in Spokane,

Washington. Was Phillips actually the infamous Butch Cassidy? Although current evidence refutes the claim that Phillips and Cassidy are the same person, it is still conceivable.

Four miles north of Globe, Wesley Goswick was a rancher with two daughters, Myrtle and Lou. On June 23, 1910, the girls, ages twelve and fourteen, died. Kingsley Olds, a hired hand, was told to drive a wagon to Horseshoe Bend to retrieve a gasoline engine that was there. The girls wanted to go along so they could stop to have a picnic by the creek. The girl's father said they were welcome to go with Olds on the trip. That evening, just before dark, Goswick became concerned when they hadn't arrived home, so he set out to look for them.

Goswick discovered bloodstains everywhere and eventually located Olds, who had been shot in the chin, but the girls had disappeared. Olds claimed that a man had attacked him and the girls. Although there was no sign that the girls had been suffocated or handled carelessly when their bodies were found, many people thought Olds had killed them. Olds repeated the story of the attack, claiming that the girls had panicked and drowned.

A trial was hastily arranged, because there were rumors that a mob was preparing to punish Olds. The jury determined that the girls' drowning was the direct result of Olds's actions. He might not have killed the girls, but he was accountable for them. He was confined to the Gila County Jail in Globe to await sentencing.

A bridge joined the courthouse and jail, which were separated by an alley. Prisoners were escorted across the bridge to the courthouse when they had to appear in court. Late one night, someone entered the courthouse, went to a room where he could see Olds's cell and, while he was sleeping, shot and killed Olds. The case remains unsolved, since the murderer was never found. Many think Goswick was responsible, seeking retribution for the deaths of his two daughters.

Author Wilson and her friends have visited the Gila County Jail numerous times and have done investigations there, and they have always encountered some kind of activity. The first time they were there, Sandy and Lisa were with Wilson. Wilson, Sandy and Lisa are the Mystic Spirits of Arizona and do investigations all over Arizona and the surrounding states. The group's first visit occurred in November 2020, and the jail was very cold. (The lobby has heating, but the jail cells do not.)

Vinnie is the founder of the AZ Paranormal Investigation and Research Society, and he got Wilson and her friends into the jail. Vinnie took them on a tour, starting on the first floor, where the men's section is located. They

A secure walkway connects the jail to the courthouse. *Darlene Wilson.*

walked through the entire area to get a feel for the place. The energy was very heavy and has been every time the group has been there.

The women's cells are located on the second floor. Although the cells appeared stark and rough, the energy in there was different. In fact, it was quite good. Sandy brought a sample of perfume, a tester bottle. She explained to the spirits in the room that they just needed to tap the top of the bottle to spray the perfume. They left the bottle in the small section of the toilet and sink, an open area just outside of the cells. It's disgusting, but it is a prison.

About ten minutes later, while walking around the area and taking pictures, the women smelled perfume. They were so happy. One or more of the spirits had touched the bottle of perfume. They did spend quite a bit of

Gila County Jail, located in Globe, Arizona. *Darlene Wilson.*

time in that area, talking to the room. Wilson had the distinct impression that some of the spirits were there because they had murdered their husbands or boyfriends who were abusive. Some were trying to save their own lives or those of their children and did the only thing they thought was possible.

On that first visit, Lisa was upstairs in the women's section, recording a video, when she whispered, "I know you're here. Could you just sparkle for me?" And all of a sudden, two orbs came flying toward her and gave her the biggest and brightest sparkle. It was so rewarding to have that confirmation from them—that they were glad the group was there. That meant so much to all of them.

On one visit, while downstairs in the men's section, Wilson had a strong feeling that a dark energy was present. She told Lisa and Sandy that she needed to leave and started walking toward the lobby. They felt the same thing and followed her out. Wilson sat down, turned around and noticed that Sandy looked different. Her cheeks were sunken in, and there were dark circles around her eyes. Wilson knew something was happening. She grabbed her phone and started recording when suddenly, Sandy flipped around and said, "Get the f— off of me, and never touch me again. I'm a happily married woman to the same man for fifty-two years." When she turned back around, she looked fine. Wilson asked her what happened, and she said a male ghost was standing right behind her and had reached around and started rubbing her cheeks. She said it was the eeriest feeling. The group has been back several times, and this has never happened again.

The women's section of the Globe Jail is located on the second floor. *Darlene Wilson.*

On Wilson's last visit in December 2022, she brought pink carnations for the female ghost. She placed them in the women's sink and told the spirits they were welcome to smell the flowers; they smelled so sweet. The group was recording on an SLS camera (see the appendix for an explanation of this equipment) and got the most magnificent photographs of the spirits smelling the flowers. At one point, Wilson asked them to touch the KII meter to change the color of its lights, and two spirits did just that.

Another historical place in Globe is the train depot. Today's building is the second depot constructed on the property, and it was built in 1916 as a stunning red-brick two-story building with elaborate cornices and windows. The main floor was the ticket office, with waiting rooms, a telegraph office and a baggage area. The district engineer's and superintendent's offices occupied the second floor.

Globe Train Station. *Darlene Wilson.*

The first train to pull into Globe was one that belonged to the Gila Valley Globe and Northern Railroad, now the Arizona Eastern Railroad. By 1910, there were both a freight and passenger trains passing through Globe, and by 1915, the Apache Trail Tours expanded passenger service in Globe. However, by the early 1950s, with the advent of automobiles, buses and airlines, railroad passenger service decreased and eventually ceased in 1954.

Molly Cornwell, an events coordinator/facility manager of Globe, Arizona, shared the following information about the train stations in Globe. The town's first passenger station was taken down to make way for this larger, newer and more beautiful station. The newer station was built on the same property, and instead of constructing an all-in-one facility, the town built three separate structures, one of which has been lost to fire within the last two decades.

The smaller building served as the freight office. It had a front office, and the entire building was used to sort all the goods that were ordered in or going out by train. And yes, part of this was receiving or shipping coffins filled with the remains of loved ones en route to their final resting places. Sadly, it was a bustling place during the Spanish flu and the First and Second World Wars. A railroad worker had the first known case of Spanish flu in Globe.

These new buildings were erected in 1916 in anticipation of the Southern Pacific route and its promotion to bring passengers from coast to coast. The only flaw in this plan was that Globe had no connectivity to Phoenix, but the Apache Trail offered wagon trains, motorcars and scenic car transport to the Phoenix station, thus completing the coast-to-coast claim.

Around 1970, Southern Pacific saw the properties as a liability and hired a local company (Mr. Brown) to destroy the roundhouse and its surrounding properties. But the company owner had the great idea to take over the depot complex properties, and he pitched the plan to the railroad with the understanding that he would operate a business, paying all taxes and insurance, and he promised to destroy the buildings when he was done. The railroad gave him a long-term destruction lease on two of the three buildings, reserving one for itself for storage, and Mr. Brown turned the train depot complex into a laundromat, gas station and car wash.

In 2004, the keys and handshake promise for the freight office (the third building that was used for storage) were given by AZERR to Kip Culver, Historic Globe Main Street's. (Kip also successfully transformed the 1910 jail into a museum and tourism operation.) The freight office was restored, and the test Doodlebug Project was underway. Now, with the proof of concept for this grand idea of Kip's for a tourism passenger line running back and forth from the casino, forward motion was given, and the deals were made to buy out Mr. Brown's "destruction" lease and to begin the restoration.

The tourism operation ran successfully until the entire rail line was sold in 2011 (it has dedicated service to the copper mines).

The Globe Downtown Association 501(c)(6) nonprofit still holds the long-term lease on the property. It continues with the restoration goals, offering the beautiful space as a venue for weddings, parties and community fundraisers. In addition, the train depot serves the industry by hosting industry film crews and paranormal investigation teams from around the world.

"We are thankful to still have her in our care," said Molly. Author Wilson has also done several investigations at the train depot. It is such a beautiful building, and yes, you can imagine the activity that once occurred there.

One paranormal incident that Wilson personally aware of occurred in 2021 in Globe. As her group left the train station and walked outside to the smaller museum, Maureen heard a man's voice say, "What? Where?" He seemed confused.

The group asked Molly Cornwell why there were flowers by the side of the road, and she shared the story of Eric. Eric, age twenty-eight, had been fatally shot by a Globe police officer. While on his patrol, the police officer stopped and was talking to a man when they were approached by a man (Eric) with a knife. Eric began advancing quickly toward the man and officer. Eric walked past the man but continued toward the officer.

The officer repeatedly commanded Eric to stop and drop the knife, but Eric ignored him and continued toward the officer. The officer kept backing

The Globe Train Station Museum building. *Darlene Wilson.*

up, and Eric kept walking toward him. The officer fired his weapon when Eric got within five feet of him. The officer and emergency personnel provided first aid, but Eric was later pronounced dead.

The group believes the confused questions asked to Maureen were from Eric. His spirit didn't know where he was or what was happening. When a tragic death occurs, a spirit can become confused about what happened.

The following day, the group gathered to have breakfast, and while they were waiting for their food, Wilson felt they should go back to the area with the flowers so Maureen could talk to Eric, explain what happened and see if there was anything they could do for him. Wilson felt Maureen was the right person to talk to him since he had reached out to her during their investigation. So, the group went back. It was amazing, emotional and rewarding at the same time.

Maureen explained what had happened—that Eric was shot because of the knife in his hand that he would not drop. The group asked Eric if he wanted to go home and if they could help him cross over, but he said, "No, I want to figure things out here."

On the group's return in November 2022, they talked to Eric again. This time, his spirit was inside the train station, and he seemed resolved about what happened to him, and he was happy to be in the train station. It felt like he had made friends with other spirits in the depot. He felt calmer, more relaxed and more accepting of what happened. The group felt very honored to have him talk to them again.

So many horrific hangings and killings are described in Globe's documented history. Naturally, these stories were typical of many other mining towns.

The Drift Inn Saloon is in what was once the International House, constructed in 1902. In the past, it has been home to various businesses, like a brothel, barbershop, grocery store, furniture store and much more, but in 1980, it became the Drift Inn Saloon, and still is today. Is it haunted? Most definitely. Billiards chalk is often seen flying across the room, and barstools are knocked over when no one is there. Some believe it's the ghost of a man who was shot by his ex-girlfriend in 1963. He was sitting at the end of the bar when she came in and shot him.

Globe is much more than the ghosts roaming its old historical buildings. It is unique because of its strong community spirit. The downtown area is home to locally owned businesses, restaurants and cafés. It is special because of its rich history and heritage. It offers a unique mix of history, culture and natural beauty.

HARSHAW

Once a thriving mining town of around two thousand people, Harshaw is now a ghost town. The ruins of one building are still evident, and the Harshaw Cemetery is still located under a giant sycamore tree. It is difficult to see the deserted mining town, knowing it was once home to many families and over two hundred buildings, homes and businesses. There is sadness felt by everyone who sees it, as they know the one ruin left standing represents part of the history of this great state. Circumstances change so quickly.

Clara Migoya, a journalist who wrote an article for *High Country News* on September 28, 2020, said it best: "Centuries-old sycamore trees tower over the dry riverbed of Harshaw Creek, in the Patagonia mountains of southern Arizona. Where houses once stood, flat, barren earth stretches to the base of nearby low oak-covered hills. A crumbling wooden building, a relic of a mining supervisor's home, and a cemetery are all that remain of what once was one of the West's richest mining towns."

The town was thought to have been a Spanish settlement and ranch before it became Harshaw. Around 1764, the Apache assaulted the settlement, and everything was destroyed. Forty-four people died in the attack on the nearby ranch.

It all began when David Tecumseh Harshaw was instructed to relocate his cattle out of the pasture where he had them grazing in the Patagonia Mountains. They were in Apache country, Indian Agent Tom Jeffords informed him. As a result, David Harshaw relocated them to the town's current location in 1877, renaming the area Harshaw in his honor after discovering a rich silver deposit there. He began operating several mines nearby; he named one Hermosa and another Hardshell. Two years later, David Harshaw moved after selling everything to a New York organization.

The town was founded in 1881, and its post office operated there between 1880 and 1903. Boardinghouses, bars, hotels, shops, blacksmiths, banks, general stores, stables, dance halls and an *Arizona Bullion* newspaper office were all there.

The mining resumed but only briefly. The New York group stopped all mining due to the decrease in the amount of high-grade silver in the mines. A fire was started by a violent storm's lightning. The town began to die as the mine's ore supply was exhausted. The remaining buildings were deserted as people began to leave.

Over the years, several individuals and businesses have held various leases on the mines in the area. Yet as silver prices dropped, the mine once again closed.

Clara Migoya wrote a great article about Harshaw and the Soto family. The Soto family grew up in Harshaw in the 1940s and '50s. Now living in Tucson, they often gather and remember their childhood days. They still have a property in Harshaw, which they knew as El Durazno, meaning "the peach." The Sotos arrived in the El Durazno area in the 1870s. The town had thirty saloons, a church, a school, shops and a post office.

When Ben Daniels, one of Roosevelt's Rough Riders, sold a mine in the Harshaw District to a business partner in 1906, Harshaw made headlines again. It appears that the mine was owned by someone other than Daniels.

The Coronado National Forest was formed in 1953, but Harshaw ran afoul of the U.S. Forest Service in 1983. Because the town's seventy residents had yet to officially receive titles to their land, the federal government referred to them as squatters. The forestry staff's efforts to relocate them and cooperate with them were unsuccessful.

When the owners arrived, all but one of the old buildings had been removed by the forestry service. The house is thought to belong to a superintendent or one of the mine owners.

Wilson and her friends Linda, Tom and Melissa paid a visit to Harshaw in November 2022, and the shell of the building and the hillside of the cemetery is still there. This beautiful, peaceful area is sad as well, because it meant so much to so many people, and now, little is left.

The group wandered up the hill to the Harshaw Cemetery. Some of the markers are difficult to see due to the growth of weeds and trees. The headstones go up a small, steep hill, and are placed among some monuments, some with trees growing around them.

The group had their recorders going as they walked through the cemetery. Linda heard children's voices laughing, as if they were playing a game of hide and seek—happy laughter, happy child spirits.

Harshaw, Arizona, with only the ruins of a building left. *Darlene Wilson.*

Harshaw Cemetery. *Darlene Wilson.*

Wilson and her friends then walked to the one remaining shell of a building that is believed to be what is left of James Finley's house. It was meant to be the superintendent's residence and was built around 1877. Wilson and her friends sat inside the structure and had their recorders going. They heard voices of people outside the building hovering by the opening that once was a side door. It felt as if they wanted to come in but were hesitant.

A young girl's voice was heard the most. She was around sixteen years old and was excited for the group to be there. She wanted to talk with them, maybe share her stories of life in Harshaw. But someone, a male voice, cautioned her to not enter. He insisted that those with him should leave—and they did.

Author Wilson is sure there are many other spirits still lingering there. The town of Harshaw was loved by many. Children were born there, and miners and their family members died there. It's only natural some may remain to remember those days past.

MIAMI

Arizona's Gila County is home to the Pinal Mountains, a mountain range with maximum elevation of 7,848 feet and a prominence of 4,000 feet. Native Pueblo people lived there around the eleventh and twelfth centuries. Around the fifteenth century, the Apache and Yavapai people started settling there. The Spanish arrived in the seventeenth century, exploring the area. But a battle was fought between the Spanish forces and local Apache warriors, now known as the Battle of the Pinal Mountains.

The Tonto Apache tribe previously lived in the region now called Miami that is surrounded by the Pinal Mountains. In the late 1860s, silver mining encouraged European colonization. These communities have a history of Apache raids to take livestock.

A group of men led by King S. Woolsey were given permission by Arizona territorial governor Goodwin to confront the Apache on January 27, 1864, to reclaim their livestock, because they had grown tired of the Apaches' frequent raids. The hostile Natives eventually surrounded them, and one white man and twenty-four Apache were slain in what became known as the Bloody Tanks Massacre.

In the 1870s, silver mining began in the region. Silver's price fell in the 1880s, but copper's price rose, and miners started showing an interest in copper. The need for men to work in the mines grew in 1906. Miami was established due to the necessity for housing for the miners and places for them to shop and find recreational activities.

When Miami was established in 1907, it had brutal streets, no utilities and eight hundred residents. In the 1910 census, Miami had a population of 1,390. Today, Miami's population is 2,168, and it is a peaceful town with antique shops filled with ancient artifacts. A large number of the structures in the downtown area are in the National Register of Historic Places. There are thirty listed, five of which are concrete Luten arch bridges that cross Bloody Tanks Wash.

The ghosts that haunt the old copper mine near the town include the spirit of an old miner who died in the mine. Strange noises have been heard coming from the mine; some have even seen the ghostly figure of the miner roaming the area.

Rita Olsen, the Arizona Ghost Adventures Group owner, shared many stories of the buildings in Miami.

One of the town's haunted places is the YMCA, which author Wilson had an opportunity to investigate. Both she and Rita had similar experiences, although they have never met. When they talked on the phone and Wilson heard about Rita's experiences in the YMCA, it was eerie, because she was describing exactly what Wilson had felt.

Rita said they walked into the pool room and down into the dry pool, where people claimed that while playing in the pool, an entity would grab their legs and pull them under.

The YMCA in Miami, Arizona. It was built in 1917 as a community building and boardinghouse. *Parker Anderson.*

In the upstairs gym room, Rita felt a lot of wartime spirits marching through. Where were they marching? No one knows.

Let's back up a bit. The YMCA was built in 1917 with a lobby, a gym with a stage, a swimming pool and rooms for rent. The building comprises 18,938 square feet and two stories and is zoned for commercial use. This is important to mention because the building is for sale. Its current owner, Barb Holtzen, is passionate about the old building. When she bought it and started renovations, which continue today, she could see what it once was and how important it was to save. But because of a divorce and later marriage, Holtzen is now living quite a distance from the building, and travel from her home to the YMCA has taken its toll. She wants to pass the torch to someone else who wishes to save this part of Arizona's history.

Barb has graciously allowed paranormal groups to come and investigate the building for a small fee. Thank goodness she is doing this, because Wilson was only able to visit Miami and the surrounding area with the help of her and Vinnie. Vinnie is the founder and lead investigator of AZ Paranormal Investigations and Research Society, and he got Wilson

The back-left corner of the YMCA's drained pool is where several of us felt vertigo. *Parker Anderson.*

entrance to the YMCA. He is also working hard to save the old buildings in Arizona's mining towns.

In December 2022, author Wilson had a group of people interested in doing an investigation at the YMCA. This was her first time there. When they entered the building, they walked into its vast lobby. Tables and chairs were set up, perfect for meetings, gatherings, weddings and more. Then they walked down a long hall with side doors into smaller rooms and the pool. It is now drained but is surprisingly huge with a deep end. As the group walked around the pool, they found back in one corner a door that led to the boiler room. In that area, Wilson started getting vertigo—so much so that she thought she would tip over into the deep end of the empty swimming pool. She couldn't wait to get out of that corner. She put her back flat against the wall and began slowly scooting along it until she got out of that room.

Although the group was told no one died in the building, that doesn't mean it isn't haunted by the spirits of those who once lived, worked or played there.

The group ventured upstairs to the kitchen and dining room area. Down the hallway, there were many smaller rooms, some that were being renovated, some that were empty and some that had their doors closed. The energy was different along the hallway; some places had heavier feelings, and others were light and airy.

In what was once the dining room, the group set up their various pieces of equipment and got amazing videos of multiple ghosts. They used an SLS (structured light sensor), a camera that projects an invisible infrared laser grid and can recognize and highlight human figures. It highlights figures by making the objects, humans or ghosts appear as bright green stick people. That's why some people call them SLS stickman cameras.

The group asked questions like, "Did you live here? Did you have your meals here? Did you play in the building?" And they got positive responses and captured children's spirits. Then in the doorway to the kitchen, a much smaller ghost appeared—that of a small child who appeared to be crawling on the floor.

While walking down the long hallway, one group member turned around very quickly, because he heard and felt someone behind him. The group searched the area with their equipment but didn't see anything; others heard the noise, too, as if someone was following them.

Sometimes, you don't always get solid proof in an investigation (like video on a camera or recorder), but you know something or someone is there. Investigators do their best to capture something to help prove the existence of ghosts/spirits, confirming the bumps in the night, the taps on the shoulder, the whispers or the breeze that sweeps past you as a spirit tries to contact you and share its story.

Another historical and haunted building in Miami is the Bullion Plaza Cultural Center and Museum. It was opened in 1923 as a grammar school. It had over twenty classrooms and a small theater/auditorium. It served as a grammar school from 1923 to 1994, when it was closed due to disrepair; it was unsafe for use as a public school.

The school, when in operation, reflected the segregation that prevailed in many Arizonan towns by serving as a school for children who were Mexican American and Apache. With high academic standards and severe discipline, the English teachers demonstrated a nearly missionary feeling of dedication. For those who disregarded the English-only regulation, physical punishment was occasionally used.

The interior of the school has been somewhat altered, but the exterior has not changed. Bullion Plaza was acquired by the Town of Miami in 1997 from the school district and was put to use as a museum and cultural center.

Bullion Plaza in Miami was built in 1923 as a school. It served as a school until 1994, and it is now a cultural museum that was listed in the National Register of Historic Places in 2001. *Rita Olsen.*

Rita Olsen and her AZ Ghost Adventures group lead and have led many investigations at the Bullion Plaza. Her stories are chilling, intriguing and informative. The area is very active with the spirits of those who once worked or went to school there.

In Rita's words: "So, we'll start with the students first. The students we have encountered on the second floor, up in one of the far corners—I call the attic room because there's a ladder that goes up there. We have many children come through. There was a photographer there, and he took a picture of me and another person standing there with me, and we have a children's ghosts come through. He took a picture of us, and a child's face shows up between us."

Rita continued:

> *There's a teacher up there also, and he probably wasn't the nicest teacher. There is a report that there was a teacher found dead in the stairwell in that area—they believe from a heart attack.*
>
> *At one point, we kept getting a name coming through—Pearl—she was one of the first Black teachers to win the Teacher of the Year award. Rita said she didn't know that, but the next morning when she met with*

Tom, the director of Bullion building, she told him about the name that kept coming up, and he said, "Come with me." He took her to a room they never go in, and Tom showed her an award in one of the cabinets for that teacher.

So, up on the second floor, Tom's office is up there. A few years back, we were doing a dowsing rod session, and Tom said he feels there is a woman who is keeping an eye on him. So, I was upstairs all by myself, and I felt someone watching me, so I turned around and started taking pictures, and when I got home and looked at the photos on my computer, you can clearly see a ghost of a woman standing next to his office door. It was like you could see through her.

We spoke to a Medium from the UK, and he knew nothing about the Bullion building. And I was walking around. He said, "You know you have a woman following you around; she's very attached to that place." And I said, "Oh, thank you." So, that comment was very validating.

We have shadow figures in the hallway—both adults and children. And we, just this past weekend, I was sitting on the floor, and it was very, very cold. And there's this metal ladder that goes up to what we call the attic, and I don't like it there. That hole going up to the top is dark.

In fact, they had someone up there working on the attic, and he came downstairs and asked if this place was haunted. He kept turning around thinking someone was there watching him.

So, this past weekend, when I was sitting on the floor, there was a woman behind me, and she had a camcorder with infrared, and she was recording towards the ladder. And she said, "Is there supposed to be a heat signature going up and down the ladder?" And I said, "Absolutely not." And it was cold in there. She showed me the video, and you can see the heat signature going down the ladder. Then I said, "Could you go back up the ladder?" And they watched the heat signature go up the ladder. It was freezing in that room. We had turned off all the lights and the breakers at the beginning, so there was no heat coming from any of us—just the ghosts.

So, something I had happened to me personally: there is a room, one of the classrooms, one of the old classrooms with the coat room and a closet in the back of the room. My son, who is six foot, four inches tall was with me on this investigation. As a young child, he's always had experiences. It was pitch dark, the only lights you could see was the red glow from the emergency exit lights. I was walking, and the door was closed to this classroom, but they have this door with long windows in the door. I was walking past the classroom, and where I was coming from—I was facing the coat room, I could see the entrance to the coat room—and all of sudden, this big black figure, darker than our room was, because the room had a reddish glow from the exit signs, and it had a white light on the front of it, and I thought it was my son carrying a flashlight or one of those headlamps, because it wasn't a huge light. It was definitely a white circle. There was a lady walking with me, and I said, "Oh, just a minute. I need to tell my son something." And I open the door, and I look in, and the room is empty. I checked the coat room, and no one was there. I said something to the lady with me, and she said, "I saw what you saw. I saw someone walking out of the coat room."

Now, we're on the landing where I saw the little girl. One of our guests had brought her teenage daughter (sixteen years old), old enough to do the investigation. She comes up to me and says she saw a little girl. I asked her, "What did she look like?" And she described exactly what I had seen.

On the main floor, there's the Slovak Room. I'm Polish and grew up in a Polish community in Chicago, so when I go in, I play music, and I get a lot of responses from that, and the spirits that come through are very cultural. We had a lady there once who spoke Bulgarian, and I said I'm getting something, but I don't understand it. The next thing you know, this lady is having a full-blown conversation with the spirit, and she's understanding their responses. There are spirits that are of Czeck, Serbian and Slovak origin.

Then we go down the hall to what is called the Native American Room. When we discuss the Hohokam and the various tribes, we'll get a lot of activity. In fact, one time it seemed like someone was running around the room.

Today, in 2023, when you visit Miami, at first glance, you see abandoned buildings and homes and empty streets, but there is more to this town. You can see the progress with the few shops that have opened and feel a sense of optimism in the air. You can feel the determination of the people who have stayed to make the town come alive again.

The people, the food and the stunning night sky with the mountains in the background make this a lovely location.

Rita Olsen is the owner and operator of AZ Ghost Adventures. She has experienced the paranormal for as long as she can remember. At the age of seven, she suffered a near-death accident and believes it is one reason she has so many experiences. She also works in healthcare with both geriatric and pediatric people.

Her philosophy is that "some people are destined to follow a certain path and have the ability to steer what direction that path leads us....My path is helping others through my work in healthcare and contributing to the community. With regards to the paranormal, I strongly feel that my purpose is to learn the stories of the spirits that I encounter and bring their stories forward."

PATAGONIA

At an altitude of 4,050 feet, Patagonia is tucked away among the Sky Islands and is home to about nine hundred people. The Coronado National Forest encircles the area, giving it a feeling of remoteness.

Sky Island refers to the mountain ranges in the Arizona area that are floating habitat islands due to their height above the clouds.

It is said that the Welsh miners who migrated here from Patagonia, South America, are thought to have given the Patagonia region its name. They started referring to the area as the Patagonia Mountains.

Natives were the first people to live in the area. They discovered that the lush terrain around the Sonoita and Harshaw Creeks was ideal for their way of life, full of hunting and fishing opportunities. Spanish explorers arrived in the region close to the Mexican border in 1539.

Patagonia, Arizona's welcome sign. *Nancy Burgess.*

Father Kino arrived in the region in 1692 as a missionary to convert the locals to Catholicism. He found Sonoita Creek in 1698 and went there to meet the Native inhabitants of the Arizona region.

It became challenging to mine or raise livestock in the area, as the Apache started conducting raids in the late 1700s. Many miners and homesteaders gave up and fled as a result of the constant attacks.

When the Gadsden Purchase was signed in 1853, mining activity in the region picked back up. Order was restored when American troops were dispatched to the region in 1856. But because of the start of the Civil War, the troops were pulled out, which allowed the Apache to resume their rampage.

In 1867, after the Civil War was over, the army was ordered back to set up a camp, and mining and ranching resumed.

"Rollin Rice" Richardson, a rancher and Civil War veteran, invested in the Patagonia Mountains region, which included mines and a ranch, in the 1890s. He paid a Tucson surveyor to draw up the settlement's boundaries. In 1899, he requested the opening of a post office and named the community Rollin in his honor. The locals opposed this and wanted the town named after the Patagonia Mountains. In 1900, Patagonia was acknowledged as the town's administrative name.

Patagonia featured three hotels, an opera theater, a schoolhouse, a two-story train depot, two parks, numerous shops and saloons and running water in 1900. As the stock market crashed in 1929, the region experienced uncertainty. Also, the summer rains contributed to floods and the destruction of most of the area's bridges. By November that year, the railroad had submitted a request for approval to cut its Patagonia–Mexico route.

Although Patagonia's economy has had ups and downs, it is steadfast in its commitment to and love for its people. The town's citizens requested incorporation in 1947; on February 10 that year, it became official.

As financial difficulties returned to Patagonia in 1957, the town's mill and power plant closed. The railroad abandoned its depot and began removing the tracks in a month. The town's primary source of income was gone.

After the last ore was shipped in 1960 and the last of the railroad line was removed in 1962, a Patagonia resident bought the depot in 1964 to keep it from being demolished. A year later, he sold it to the local Rotary Club, which began restoring it. The station grounds were donated to the town and made into a town park in 1966. The restored depot is now the municipal offices of Patagonia.

Today, the town park is a favorite place for locals to enjoy quiet walks, family picnics and annual festivals. Oak and willow trees line the park,

OLD RAILROAD STATION · PATAGONIA, ARIZONA

Patagonia's old railroad station. *Nancy Burgess.*

providing shade in the summer and stunning autumn colors in the fall. Walking along the park, you will notice shops, galleries and restaurants you can explore.

Patagonia Lake was established in 1968 after a dam was erected south of the town, and it became a state park in 1974. It is a man-made reservoir just southwest of the town of Patagonia. It is now a popular area for boating and sport fishing. There are camping areas, picnic areas, tables, grill areas and cabins you can rent. Visit the Arizona State Park website for more information about this park.

Today, hikers, international bird-watchers and cyclists congregate in or stay the night in Patagonia. A gravel cyclist's paradise, the Arizona Trail is biker friendly. An outdoor restaurant, the Cyclists Menu, has a bike shop and space heaters for winter weather, and it is a place where riders congregate. A board outside the restaurant lists the cycling regulations. On a Saturday morning when Wilson and her friends were in Patagonia, the cyclists gathered to sip coffee, chat with friends and get ready for their adventure.

Wilson and her friends fell in love with the town, its people and the region's stunning beauty on their trip to Patagonia in November 2022. When they arrived in town, it was late at night, and they passed a building called Velvet Elvis La Mision. The next morning, of course, they had to check it out. They had the privilege of meeting the owner, Cecilia San Miguel, a beautiful woman with an incredible imagination and a strong belief in following your heart and vision. "The universe will support you," Cecilia said. And it does.

Walking through the doors, you are transported to another world—a world of color, history and mystical beauty like no other in Arizona. You come to an abrupt stop, mouth wide open, stunned into silence at the impressive grandness of this five-thousand-square-foot restaurant.

Top: The Patagonia restaurant Velvet Elvis. *Bottom*: Velvet Elvis's stunning interior. *Darlene Wilson.*

You are greeted by the most stunning wood carving of the archangel Michael, the spiritual warrior in the battle of good versus evil. The enormous room has different sitting areas, a comfortable sofa, table and chairs and brilliant, colorful murals and art. In the back of the sitting area is the most impressive bar.

The menu has everything from salads and freshly baked breads to calzones and stromboli, designer pizzas and mouth-watering desserts. Check out the website for more information about the Velvet Elvis at La Mision: https://www.velvetelvislamision.com/.

One story Cecilia shared with us was that while the construction was ongoing, she had a small apartment built inside the restaurant, where she lived. At night, when it was very cold, she would put on her long white fur coat to keep herself warm. She'd walk around the restaurant, inspecting everything and making plans for what she wanted to be done. The group joked that people walking through the park late at night might have seen the lady in white wandering around the restaurant, but they said that renovations really do agitate the spirits.

Haunted? With this much history? Most definitely. The paranormal activity Wilson heard about came from people who were visiting the area. They reported experiencing strange activity, like shadows hanging around the old train depot.

Although there is no evidence to suggest that Patagonia is haunted, the surrounding abandoned mining camps, towns and cemeteries do experience activity.

PEARCE

In 1895, Jimmie Pearce rode his horse up a hill, dismounted and rested. He started picking at the pieces of quartz, hammering on a few, and a small piece broke loose, revealing gold. Pearce had discovered a rich grade of gold.

Jimmie named his find the Commonwealth and staked out five claims, one for each of his family members.

Back in Tombstone, Jimmie and his wife were a frugal and hardworking couple. He worked as a miner, and she ran a boardinghouse. Between the two, they saved enough money to invest in a cattle ranch in the Sulphur Springs Valley fifty miles from Pearce. Their sons had always wanted to live on a ranch; they wanted to be cowboys.

This mine was unique in that when earlier prospectors were mining the area in the 1870s, they overlooked this area. It was just waiting for the right person to find it. And he did.

Pearce was hounded by eager promoters who wanted to get their hands on the rich mine. Finally, Pearce worked with a banker from New Mexico, John Brockman, who made him a deal. If Brockman could pay Jimmie $250,000 in gold ore within a designated period, Pearce would sell the land to him. Sixty days later, the Commonwealth Mine had a new owner.

Mrs. Pearce had been operating the only boardinghouse in Pearce, and before she would sign over her rights to the mine, she wanted a guarantee that she would have exclusive rights to continue running the boardinghouse at the mine. Brockman agreed.

After that, the town of Pearce grew quickly. Residents from Tombstone began dismantling their homes and businesses and packing them over to the new town. By 1919, the town had an excellent school, saloons, hotels, restaurants and a movie theater. The post office (which is still standing) was established in 1896. The mine had several different owners. In 1905, it experienced many challenges and setbacks. A mine cave-in in 1904 caused flooding and the decline of the ore's value.

Although it continued to produce until 1910, when defective wiring destroyed the mill, the mine was bought by another company and operated into the 1920s. Overall, mines produced millions of ounces of silver and gold. There are varying stories of the exact amount produced—like a "fish tale." But the mine was extremely successful and provided a living for hundreds of miners and their families.

Burt Alvord was the deputy for Pearce, Arizona. It was only a short time before Alvord became an outlaw and formed his gang. They robbed trains throughout the Arizona Territory. They would use the town of Pearce as their headquarters.

Bill Downing, another outlaw in the area, became a member of the Alvord Gang, and together, they robbed the Cochise Train Station. Downing was eventually captured, tried and sentenced to prison in the Yuma Territorial Prison.

John Peters Ringo, who was born in May 1850 and died in July 1882, was known as Johnny Ringo, an outlaw who took part in Mason County War in Texas. In 1882, Ringo was in Tombstone, where he traded threats with Doc Holliday. Both were arrested and hauled before a judge for carrying weapons in town. They were fined and released. But during a follow-up trial, the judge found outstanding charges against Ringo for a robbery. Ringo was rearrested and jailed. The Earps always believed that Ringo took part in the ambush of Virgil Earp that crippled him for life and the murder of Morgan Earp.

Johnny Ringo was found dead, propped against a tree and shot through the head. There were many speculations about his death. Did he die by suicide, or was he murdered? There were newspaper reports that said Ringo frequently threatened suicide and that the event was expected at any time. One story says ranch hands found his body up against a tree with a gun beside him—but all the bullets were still in the gun.

A historic Pearce mercantile store. *Linda Dershem.*

Wyatt always claimed he shot Ringo. He told his story many times, but in one account, he denied having killed Ringo. What was the truth? No one living knows for sure.

Like they did in so many other mining towns in Arizona, when the mine closed in the 1930s, people began to move away. Now, the town is reduced to a post office, a country store/museum, a few homes and a cemetery.

The cemetery of Pearce was formalized by President Woodrow Wilson when he deeded forty acres to the Pearce Lodge 21 of the Knights of Pythias. The earliest identified graves date to the late 1890s. Burials stopped in the 1960s.

Buried at the cemetery is George Hart Platt, who was born in 1832 and died in 1906 at the age of seventy-three or seventy-four. He enlisted on December 8, 1863, as a quartermaster sergeant in the Union Light Guard, Ohio Cavalry. Rhonda Reid of the Sierra Vista Paranormal Group found some interesting information on Platt. He was a member of the Union Light Guard of Ohio, which was formed for the express purpose of acting as bodyguard to the president of the United States—at that time, President Lincoln. There is a sign in the cemetery that says, "Bodyguard to President Lincoln," but it has no name.

Another famous resident of Pearce Cemetery is Antonio Palma Sr. (1883–1927). He was a champion driller for the Commonwealth Mine. The rock he drilled for the competition sits at the cemetery entrance.

A local shared one story with author Wilson about Our Lady of Victory Catholic Church. The church was constructed of adobe. Its ceiling and interior walls are made of plaster, and it has hardwood floors. It was

Pearce Cemetery. *Darlene Wilson.*

built in 1916. It was classified as a station church, which meant it had no resident priest and instead had a visiting priest who would hold services in the building. The church was seldom used in the 1930s, and little is known of the church's history from the '40s and '50s. In 1961, it was no longer in use. By 1963, the church was back in service, with the town of Sunsites nearby. But in 1969, the Diocese of Tucson sold the building to a private party.

The story the local shared with Wilson came from the mid-1930s, when they were a child. While sneaking out of the house at night, they stopped when they saw lights moving around in the church. No one should have been there, but someone was. They crept outside the church, looking inside when they could and spotted the light in midair, but no one was holding it. That scared them so much that they no longer left their house late at night or went near the church.

When leaving Pearce late at night, watch out for the ghostly hitchhiker. He is said to be a former resident who died in a car accident, and he is often seen wearing a white shirt and jeans, looking for a ride.

RUBY

Arizona has so many mining towns, but few have a past as bloody and creepy as Ruby's. Mining was started in the Montana Mountains area in the 1700s by the Spaniards. Their mining was rough and quick, so when the American prospectors arrived in the area in 1877, the grounds were uneven, with huge holes and hills of dirt.

From the 1880s to 1896, tremendous progress was made with road and water resource development. In 1897, Julius Andrews operated the Montana Camp General Store. In 1912, the post office was established, changing the name of Montana Camp to Ruby, the name of Andrews's wife, Lillie B. Ruby Andrews.

In 1913, Phil Clarke bought the Ruby General Store. In 1915, he moved the store, post office and living quarters up the hill on land that he had purchased there in Ruby. Clarke moved his wife and children to Tucson, as he was concerned for his family's safety, living so close to the Mexican border. With the withdrawal of the soldiers and the protection they offered, Clarke felt uneasy. In 1919, Clarke sold the general store to the Fraser brothers.

John and Alexander Fraser signed the final papers for the general store on February 16, 1920, and fifteen days later, they were both dead. On February 27, 1929, two Mexican bandits robbed and brutally murdered the Fraser brothers.

In the early morning of Friday, February 27, 1929, Alexander was opening the store as usual, getting everything ready for a busy day, when a Mexican

Ruby Mill's foundation and mining area still remain. *Darlene Wilson.*

Ruby, Arizona's town sign. *Darlene Wilson.*

bandit named Lara entered the store and shot Alexander in the back. John was in the back room. Hearing the shot, he ran to the front of the store and saw his brother Alexander on the floor, shot in the back, with the bandit Lara standing over him. Lara and his accomplice, Garcia, ordered John to open the safe; they cleaned it out and then shot John in the eye.

When County Ranger Parmer arrived at the scene, he wasn't prepared for the grisly sight. Alexander was shot in the back and in the head. John was shot through the left eye, and the bullet passed through his skull, but John was still alive, and he could identify the two bandits.

Innes Fraser, John's wife, was in San Diego with their four children when she was notified by telegraph of the shooting in Ruby. Three telegrams arrived stating what happened, and they said someone needed to come take care of the business. Another said her husband requested she go to him at the hospital, and another telegram stated his condition was severe and to take the stage from Tucson to Nogales.

Innes, the couple's youngest daughter and her sister arrived at the hospital, but it was too late. John Fraser had passed away that morning. After the funeral, which was delayed so all of John's family could come, Innes turned the store over to the previous owner, Phil Clarke, and left for San Diego.

The search for the killers continued, and in October that year, Garcia was found and arrested by Deputy McLure. Garcia overpowered the deputy, grabbed a gun hidden under his pillow and shot Deputy McLure. Deputy Holloway wrestled with Garcia; the man broke away and staggered back, and both deputies shot Garcia, killing him. Deputy McLure survived his gunshot wound and received a letter of concern from Innes Fraser. Lara never returned to the United States but was arrested on a murder charge and was imprisoned in Sonora, Mexico.

Frank Pearson approached Phil Clarke to buy the store. Clarke tried to talk him out of it because of the murders that had taken place the previous month, but he was determined to buy it. Frank Pearson moved his wife and four-year-old daughter, Margaret, to Ruby and opened the store.

Frank and Myrtle were from Texas and were farmers there, but because of his health, they moved to Arizona; they tried several towns before settling in Ruby. As the previous store owners, they lived in the back rooms. Myrtle was also a teacher in Texas, so she taught in the one-room school in Ruby and helped in the store. The town's population at that time was around 50, but 218 lived in the surrounding areas, and all the children attended the school.

Ruby Mercantile store ruins. It was the site of two murders in 1920 and 1921. *Darlene Wilson.*

A year and a half later, Frank and Myrtle were murdered by Mexican bandits. Frank was in the store with his sister Irene Pearson, who was visiting from Texas. Elizabeth Purcell, Myrtle's sister, was visiting from Texas as well. When Irene's back was turned, she heard her brother get shot. She took off running back to the living quarters when two of the seven bandits chased her, grabbed her and dragged her back to the store.

Myrtle was upstairs with their daughter Margaret when they heard shots from the store. Myrtle took off running downstairs, screaming Frank's name. Margaret said that as she ran to the store, one of the bandits took off after her. When she fell, the bandit turned and went back. Her aunt Elizabeth saw her and quickly got her out to a bunkhouse.

Margaret recalled hearing that her mother's gold teeth had been knocked out of her mouth by a rifle butt. Her aunt Elizabeth was in the bedroom when a bandit shot at her. The bullet hit her hand, and she fainted, so he left her.

Irene, Elizabeth and Margaret left the area for the hills, where they hid for several hours. They went back down and found no one at the store except for the bodies of Frank and Myrtle.

The bandits had taken all the money from the safe and robbed the store of all its shoes, clothing, food and mail. They had also cut the telephone wires so that help could not be called.

When the law officers arrived, George Camphuis and his wife had already reached the store from a mine two miles west of Ruby. The Camphuises got busy dealing with the bodies, washing and dressing them.

144

Ruby School, now the Ruby Museum. *Darlene Wilson.*

Irene Purcell told the officers that three bandits had committed the shooting and that the others had remained outside, standing guard. Three Mexican women who were neighbors of the Pearsons identified Silvas and Martinez as two of the bandits.

The officers took Irene, Elizabeth and young Margaret to Nogales, where Irene wired her father and Myrtle's brother. When all of their family had arrived, the bodies of Frank and Myrtle were taken by train to Texas for burial. Irene, Elizabeth and Margaret went on the train with their family.

A massive manhunt was underway for the murdering bandits. A $5,000 reward poster dated August 26, 1921, was offered for the persons who murdered the postmaster and family in Ruby, Arizona. It read, "Seven Mexican Bandits Participated in This Crime" and that the post office department would pay any person who brought in mail robbers.

Silvas was captured for disturbing the peace about thirty-five miles from Ruby in September 1921. At his trial, the Pearsons' Mexican neighbors testified that Silvas was with Martinez and they saw them going into and leaving the mercantile store in Ruby. Irene Pearson returned to Nogales from Texas to testify that Silvas was the one who fired the first shot at her brother. At the same time, word came that Martinez had been arrested earlier and deported to the United States from Nogales. Martinez made a full confession and named Silvas as one of the bandits who raided the Ruby store.

Martinez was found guilty, and in August 1923, he was hanged at the Florence Penitentiary for the murder of Frank Pearson. Silvas was found guilty and sentenced to life in prison. Because of good behavior, he was put on the "Outside Trusty" list, and in 1928, he escaped from the ranch, never to be seen again.

In 1926, Eagle-Picher Lead Company took the option to buy the Montana Mine (Ruby) and did many things to improve mining in that area. The company mined there from 1928 to 1940, when the ore ran out. The post office closed in 1941, and the school was closed in 1946. At that time, Ruby became a ghost town.

Richard Frailey and five other people from Tucson, Arizona, bought Ruby as a real estate investment. They had plans to make Ruby a place to relax, fish and hunt. They had to post "No Trespassing" signs to keep out unwanted visitors. With the death of Frailey, they leased the property to Tech Associates, which wanted the tailings. They also reaped some rewards but not enough to pay expenses. Other companies held leases, but none were successful. Since 1990, there has been no more mining at Ruby.

On May 6, 1975, the ghost town of Ruby was put in the National Register of Historic Places. That also made Ruby eligible for the Grants-in-Aid Program. It took eighteen years for the town's owners to take advantage of the program. In 1993, Pat Frederick, the daughter of Frailey, who died in 1975, and Ned and Jim Daugherty, the sons of the original owner Daugherty, worked in the town and were awarded a two-year grant.

A caretaker was needed. There have been several, but the one there today is Leslie, who planned to stay for only six months. She wanted to leave before the bats took off. Yes, bats. Bat Conservation International came to watch the old mine shaft, where 190,000 Mexican free-tailed bats lived. Leslie has settled in and enjoys the sunsets, the peace and quiet, playing her guitar and meeting the visitors.

People are welcome to visit Ruby with a reservation. The road can be quite rough. Check the town's website for more information: https://www.rubyaz.com.

In November 2022, Wilson and her friends Tom, Melissa and Linda spent the day in Ruby. They were there to investigate the old ruins, explore the grounds and see if ghosts still lingered there. They were satisfied.

They first visited the Andrewses' place—or what was left of it. The Andrewses had the first store in Ruby. Not much is left of the store, just part of a wall, but the activity there was very strong. When Melissa walked around to the right side of the wall, her batteries died. Everything died. She borrowed Wilson's battery pack to be able to get readings in that area.

While in that area, the group felt many spirits with them. The Pearsons were there, as was another couple who was murdered at their store just up

Right: Ruby ghost town caretaker, Leslie. *Darlene Wilson.*

Below: The remains of the Andrews home and the first store. *Darlene Wilson.*

Ruby Jail, built in 1936. *Linda Dershem.*

the hill. Wilson asked the Pearsons if their daughter Margaret was with them, and they said, "No." They said she had saved herself and was in a happier place.

There is a story of the jail and its ghosts of former prisoners. Although Wilson did not find any records of prisoners dying there, they could still haunt the jail from their experiences there or their guilt from what got them arrested.

The Pearsons' store, where two of them died, is said to be haunted by its former customers. Ghosts have been seen in that area, and strange noises have been heard at night. It is across the road from the jail, so the spirits might be those of the men who robbed from the store and were arrested.

These are just a few of the many ghost stories and legends that surround Ruby, Arizona. Whether you believe in the paranormal, the town's rich history and spooky tales make it a fascinating destination for ghost hunters and history buffs alike. So, if you're ever in the area, why not take a walk around the ghost town and see if you can catch a glimpse of one of Ruby's many ghosts? Who knows what you might discover in this haunted and historic town.

TOMBSTONE/BRUNCKOW CABIN

There is not much to say about Tombstone in Cochise County, "the town too tough to die," that has not already been said. The town has developed a legendary and almost mythical reputation in the annals of Southwest history. Countless books, magazine articles and, in the modern era, movies, television shows and web pages have been dedicated to it, all with varying degrees of accuracy—and many with no accuracy at all.

A number of stories exist about how the town got its unusual name, but the most accepted one is that when wildcat miner Ed Schieffelin went prospecting in the desert in that area, acquaintances told him there was nothing out there and that the only thing he would find was his tombstone. When Schieffelin eventually struck a rich silver vein, he remembered this jibe and named his mine the Tombstone. The claim was filed on September 3, 1877.

Other miners came into the area, and more rich silver lodes were struck. As they always did, a town grew up around the mine to serve the needs of the miners, and it was named Tombstone. The population grew rapidly; at its peak, the town had over fourteen thousand citizens, and it became the county seat in 1881. Tombstone became a boom town and had hotels, schools, medical facilities, saloons and live theaters.

Making a long story short, trouble began brewing as the town was divided into camps, with average citizens and mining capitalists on one side and nearby ranchers, many of whom were still Confederate sympathizers, on the other. A group of loosely organized cattle rustlers, known today as "the Cowboys," found a lucrative market among ranchers for cattle stolen in nearby Mexico and rustled across the border.

Most mining boom towns were wild, and Tombstone was no exception. Violent incidents, including shootings and other depredations, became common. Everything climaxed on October 26, 1881, with the Gunfight at the OK Corral, a now-legendary event that, over the last 140 years, has been recounted in numerous ways—to the point that people still argue about what really happened and who the good and bad guys were.

This book's authors will not try to sort out the details here. Suffice it to say that Deputy U.S. Marshal Virgil Earp, his brothers Wyatt and Morgan and gunman Doc Holliday apparently attempted to arrest members of the Clanton Gang, local ranchers who were on the Cowboys' side. Gunfire erupted, and when the smoke cleared, three men were dead: brothers Tom and Frank McLaury and Billy Clanton.

Mining continued unabated in Tombstone. Reportedly, during their heyday, the various Tombstone mines yielded over 32 million troy ounces of silver, making it the richest mining district in the history of Arizona.

After three major fires in town and other setbacks, as well as the plummeting price of silver, mining in the area began to peter out in the 1890s. Mines began closing, and citizens started leaving in droves. It's supposed that the only thing that kept Tombstone from becoming a ghost town was the fact that it was the county seat. This saved the town until 1929, when the county seat was moved to Bisbee.

But by 1929, public interest and fascination with Old West history had begun in earnest, and Tombstone began to successfully parlay this into a lucrative business. Today, Tombstone has a population of just over one thousand, and its major source of income is tourism. Every year, thousands of visitors flock here to walk the same streets where Wyatt Earp, Doc Holliday and others once lived. Annual festivals are held here to celebrate Tombstone's history.

Like so many towns that were marred by violence, Tombstone is reportedly very haunted. Often, paranormal investigators, or "ghost hunters," hold investigations of such famed buildings as the Bird Cage Theater and the OK Corral. They usually always get readings on their equipment, and the restless spirits can be rather feisty here.

Boothill Graveyard

The old cemetery now universally known by its nickname of Boothill is Tombstone's original cemetery. It got its moniker because many of the town's victims of violence were buried here, including the men who died in the gunfight at the OK Corral. Also buried here was Newman Haynes "Old Man" Clanton, the patriarch of the Clanton family who many also thought was the leader of the Cowboys.

Some tourists come away from Boothill thinking it is fake, because the city has made the decision to keep it looking like a nineteenth-century burial ground, with wooden headboards for markers and hand-printed epitaphs. But this is indeed the original Tombstone Cemetery, and as such, it has also developed a reputation for being haunted.

Paranormal investigators have generally not been allowed to hold sessions at Boothill out of respect for the dead. This has unfortunately not stopped some of the more unethical investigators from jumping the fence and poking around with their equipment. Be warned: if you do this and are caught, you *will* be arrested. Don't do it.

Brunckow Cabin

Mining engineer Frederick Brunckow was born in Germany and immigrated to the United States around 1850. To start his own mining business, which he called the San Pedro Silver Mine, Brunckow left the mining company where he was employed in 1859. Eight miles to the southwest of the future city of Tombstone, Arizona, Brucknow set up his claim. A cook born in Germany, a scientist and two miners joined him in this mining attempt. Brunckow also engaged Mexican laborers for the mining.

One of the miners went to the closest fort on July 23, 1860, to buy flour. On the evening of July 26, he returned and discovered his cousin lying on the floor, presumably murdered. The store had been plundered, with supplies and gold missing. To alert the soldiers, the miner went back to the fort. The following morning, when the soldiers came, they found two more bodies. The body of Brunckow was discovered close to the mine shaft's entrance, while the chemist's body was found partially devoured by animals not far from the camp. A rock drill had been used to kill Brunckow. The cook and the Mexican laborers were missing. The cook returned to camp later saying the Mexican laborers had released him because he was Catholic.

As one story goes, the Mexican laborers violently revolted and killed Brunckow, plowing a rock drill into his gut and throwing him down the mine shaft. What caused his workers to kill him? Maybe they realized the Brunckow land had been discovered by the Mexicans first. Or maybe Brunckow was so ambitious, he became abusive to his laborers.

From March 1863 to November 1865, Milton B. Duffield was the first U.S. marshal appointed to the Arizona Territory, and he was the new owner of the Brunckow mining claim and land, which had been transferred to him in 1873. James T. Holmes also filed a claim to the Brunckow mining claim and land on June 5, 1874. Duffield arrived at the Brunckow cabin under orders to remove Holmes. Duffield began yelling and gesturing by waving his hands and arms in his usual fashion. With Duffield's history of violence and the assumption that he was armed, Holmes grabbed his double-barreled shotgun, marched out the front door and shot the elderly lawman to death. Holmes realized his victim was not armed.

Duffield was laid to rest at the cabin, and Holmes was taken into custody, charged with murder and given a three-year prison term. Before he could serve any of his sentences, Holmes escaped. He was never again spotted in Arizona, but little effort was put into finding him.

There have been numerous claims to the Brunckow claim. Sidney R. DeLong, along with N.M. Rogers and Tom Jeffords, filed a relocation notice to get the title to the property in late 1875. Rogers was killed by Apache along with two others nearby. DeLong abandoned the claim and its buildings.

Brunckow Cabin sat empty until 1877, when Ed Schieffelin, a prospector known as the father of Tombstone, made it his permanent camp and used it as a base for exploring. Schieffelin, his brother and a fellow prospector named Gird searched the area for a week on the lookout for hostile Apache. However, they did find fresh graves that indicated recent Apache raids.

When Wilson and her friends visited Brunckow Cabin, a new fence had been put up, making it very difficult to get to the cabin. The side road is a very long and hot hike to the cabin. The group took pictures from the road to respect the historical area. After all, it is known as "the bloodiest cabin in Arizona."

Brunckow Cabin is renowned for its paranormal activity. Several people have recounted the legends passed down over the years of ghostly apparitions haunting the home and grounds, and it is reported that numerous burial sites are nearby. According to the old newspapers, between 1860 and 1881, there were seventeen to twenty-one additional fatalities on the property.

According to a May 20, 1881 article in *Prescott's Arizona Democrat*, miners skipped exploring at the Brunckow site because they had heard that tormented ghostly apparitions were haunting the home and grounds.

Occasionally, the sounds of mining equipment can be heard, including drills, axes and saws being used to cut wood.

Brunckow Cabin's ruins near Tombstone. *Darlene Wilson.*

Brunckow Cabin and its sign. *Darlene Wilson.*

Given the terrible tales and numerous killings that occurred here, one can only imagine the ghosts that haunt the location. Unsettling things like hearing unusual noises in the dark or seeing enigmatic figures in the nighttime can occur. Keep an open mind when visiting known haunted places. There is a chance that spirits are here because of this region's history.

Equipment Used in Our Investigations

CAMERAS: You can use cameras, even the camera on your cellphone, in investigations. You'll want to have your flash on and always take at least three pictures. If there is a reflection, it will show up in all your pictures. If there is a ghost, it will show up only in one.

DOWSING RODS: Everything on Earth emits energy, and dowsing rods have been used by people to tap into this energy. You can ask questions or walk around and area and see when your rods react by crossing and forming an X. Or they will swing in or out signaling "yes" or "no."

EMF DETECTOR OR KII METER: Measures EMF (electromagnetic field) and detects high spikes in particular areas and paranormal activity. When a ghost is near, the lights will change colors from green to red.

IR CAMCORDERS: Use infrared night vision recorders to record videos and document your experiences and investigations.

PENDULUMS: Similar to dowsing rods, a pendulum will swing right, left or not move at all when you ask a question. You calibrate your pendulum to show you "yes" or "no." You always pick out your own pendulum, not accepting one as a gift. It is a very personal, and you'll know the right one when you see it.

RECORDER: EVPs (electronic voice phenomena) are recorded using digital recorders. Verify the date, time and location when starting an investigation. When asking questions of the spirits in the room, allow space between questions to give spirits time to answer. You won't hear their responses until you play the recordings back.

SLS CAMERA/APP: An SLS (structured light sensor) has an infrared light projector that allows you to detect spirit forms by depicting them as stick figures.

SPIRIT BOX/GHOST BOX: This device sweeps quickly between AM or FM radio frequencies, producing a white noise that, when spirits speak, you can hear them very distinctly. It allows communications to occur in real time.

BIBLIOGRAPHY

Anderson, Parker. *Arizona Gold Gangster Charles P. Stanton: Truth & Legend in Yavapai's Dark Days*. Charleston, SC: The History Press, 2020.

Anderson, Parker, and Darlene Wilson. *Haunted Prescott*. Charleston, SC: The History Press, 2018.

Arizona Genealogy Trails. "Mines of Arizona." https://genealogytrails.com.

Ascarza, William. "Mine Tales: Congress Mine Was Golden Goose." *Arizona Daily Star*, December 30, 2013.

Garcez, Antonio R. *Arizona Ghost Stories*. Placitas, NM: Red Rabbit Press, 2018.

Gessert, Phillip (owner). "Cochise Hotel in Cochise, Arizona." https://cochisehotel.net.

Heatwole, Thelma. *Ghost Towns and Historical Haunts in Arizona*. Washington, D.C.: Primer Pub, 1981.

Inquest upon the Body of Claude M. Harvey. May 3, 1935. Arizona State Library and Archives, box 36, file 1491.

Legends of America. "Arizona Ghost Towns and Mining Camps." https://www.legendsofamerica.com/az-ghosttowns/.

Migoya, Clara. *High Country News*, September 28, 2020.

Ring, Bob, Al Ring and Tallia Pfrimmer Cahoon. *Ruby, Arizona: Mining, Mayhem, and Murder*. Tucson, AZ: U.S. Press and Graphics, 2005.

Ruelas, Richard. "In Yarnell Fire's Path, a Shrine Is Scarred but Still Standing." *Arizona Republic*, April 19, 2014.

Sherman, James E., and Barbara H. Sherman. *Ghost Towns of Arizona.* Norman: University of Oklahoma Press, 1969.

Stansfield, Charles A., Jr. *Haunted Arizona: Ghost and Strange Phenomena of the Grand Canyon State.* Mechanicsburg, PA: Stackpole Books, 2010.

Town of Clifton Arizona. "Clifton History." https://cliftonaz.com.

Varney, Phillip. *Arizona Ghost Towns and Mining Camps.* Phoenix: Arizona Highways, 2005.

Western Mining History. "Arizona Mining Towns." https://westernmining history.com.

Willson, Roscoe G. "Congress Junction Ghost Town Yields Loot in Underground Passage." *Arizona Republic,* July 15, 1951.

ABOUT THE AUTHORS

Darlene Wilson has lived in Arizona for over twenty-five years and has been involved in the paranormal world for over forty-five years as a medium and telepath. She has worked with the police in Colorado on several cases before experiencing her own ghostly encounter at the Stanley Hotel in Estes Park, Colorado, in 1989. She is the owner and tour guide of A Haunting Experience Tours/Haunted Prescott Tours in Prescott, Arizona. She coauthored *Haunted Prescott* with Parker Anderson for Arcadia Publishing/The History Press. She is the co-owner of Mystic Spirits of Arizona, a paranormal investigation team, with co-owners Sandy Munz and Lisa Stephenson.

Parker Anderson is an Arizona native and a recognized historian in Prescott and the surrounding area. He has authored the books *Elks Opera House, Cemeteries of Yavapai County, Grand Canyon Pioneer Cemetery, Wicked Prescott, Arizona Gold Gangster Charles P. Stanton* and *Hidden History of Prescott, Haunted Prescott* (with Darlene Wilson) for Arcadia Publishing/The History Press, as well as two self-published books, *Story of a Hanged Man* and *The World Beyond*. He has also authored a number of Arizona-themed history plays for Blue Rose Theater in Prescott.

FREE eBOOK OFFER

Scan the QR code below, enter your e-mail address and get our original Haunted America compilation eBook delivered straight to your inbox for free.

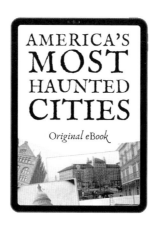

ABOUT THE BOOK

Every city, town, parish, community and school has their own paranormal history. Whether they are spirits caught in the Bardo, ancestors checking on their descendants, restless souls sending a message or simply spectral troublemakers, ghosts have been part of the human tradition from the beginning of time.

In this book, we feature a collection of stories from five of America's most haunted cities: Baltimore, Chicago, Galveston, New Orleans and Washington, D.C.

SCAN TO GET
AMERICA'S MOST HAUNTED CITIES

Having trouble scanning? Go to:
biz.arcadiapublishing.com/americas-most-haunted-cities